Awa' th' Rough Hills an' Awa'

by

Robbie Kennedy Bennett

Poetic Writing of Robbie Kennedy Bennett
since 1989
www.rkbpoetry.co.uk

ISBN-13: 978-1500868864

Awa' th' Rough Hills an' Awa' ©

2013

Awa' th' Rough Hills
where once I did play,
awa' the Rough Hills an' awa'

where are th' Rough Hills
where once I did wake
where are th' Rough Hills do they say?

Awa' th' Rough Hills
where once I leave
awa' the Rough Hills an' awa'

where are th' Rough Hills?
where once did I say
th' Rough Hills is where I am frae

For my Family
"Lang may yer lum reek"

Introduction;

Poetic pages of time in rhyme from someone with a BLACK COUNTRY and SCOTTISH ancestral background. The common decency of the honest working men that I have toiled alongside and my good family values are all I need to help put my thoughts into words.

There came a time in my life when I looked back as well as forward. Because of my parents I have always thought of myself as being half-Scottish. I was schooled and raised in the town I was born in and played football on most of the football pitches in the area. I also trained myself to be marathon fit by running many miles on roads where generations of my family have travelled and passing by factories that they have worked in. I was a very active young lad and the Royal Hospital, now redundant, was often having me as a patient. As kids my friends and I were finding out who we were when cutting our teeth in the streets and on the local playing fields around the

Rough Hills. 'I'm English but I'm also half-Scottish' I would proudly say, 'my dad is from Scotland.' In later years not only did I want to know more about my roots, I wished that I could turn back the sporting clock.

My parents had met in Aldershot Military Hospital whilst in the army and settled in my mothers home town of Wolverhampton. It was here in 1984 that I ran my first marathon. Although proud of my Wulfrunian roots and up bringing, I have always felt that there is more to me.

My dad had died in 1986 aged 59 and we knew very little of his family background. I myself was busy wrapped up at the time with being a young family man. I was also very focussed on football and running. It was late in the 1980's or early 90's whilst working at Yale Material Handling in Wednesfield when I started putting people or places into verse. Character's in life have always interested me therefore I decided to start writing. I also consider it important to explain to the reader and to remind myself years later, why I wrote the poem.

Give or take a couple of jobs and a few months, the first decade of my working life was spent at Delta Metal, Bilston Road, Wolverhampton, where there was many characters to be found and some of them I was to write about. Here are a collection of odes and their descriptions of my early days of the late 1950's and through the 60's and early 70's in Rough Hills and Parkfields area of Wolverhampton.

Poetry Titles

Wee Robie

Owen's of All Saints

Brown Tanned Arms

Letters From Louisiana

SARAH ANN AND THE SEPTEMBER SKY

I Never Knew Him as Grandad

A TRIBUTE TO NAN AND GRANDAD

The Rowley Name

Shadow of All Saints

A Little Boys Prayer

A SEA of ALL SAINTS MEMORIES

My Childhood Playground

Bridgnorth On The Severn

The Dixon Street Embankment

Down on Durberville Road

Ruts in the Dirt Road on Rooker Avenue

When The Fair Came to Parkfield Road

OUR CASTLES WERE TALL

AS THE SEA FRONT WALL

Fred Lowbridge

When Peter Said Goodbye

Hilton Road Youth Club at Hilton Hall

TURN BACK TIME

The Pretty Flower Bed at Thompson Avenue

Old Len Muir Was Funny

The Right to Stand Tall

A Personality by The Name of
Frenchie Pearson

Her Dad Disapproved

The Day of The Pub

I Once Was a Sedgley Rover

My Bloody Bilston Début

OUR WILLIE

Her Little Lips

A Fifty Something Me

A Man Should Earn

My Christmas Paper Chain

We Couldn't Catch Ray!

ALF TUPPER

THE TOUGH OF THE TRACK

MY FAMILY MY TREASURE

My Gag

The Sand of Life

My Bilston Belle

Roger Salter, an Innocent Man

Laughing in the Tavern

My Beautiful Queen

I Am Me And Not Another

A writer has to start somewhere, so I'll start in Norway 2009

Relaxing in my hotel room in Trondheim, Norway in 2009 thinking about my past.

One memory is painful, when 6 years old following my elder brother and cousin climbing onto a wall when on holiday in Gt Yarmouth, then waking up as I was being wheeled into hospital.

And a happier photo of me in my new pedal car that I had for Christmas. My elder brother is standing aside with his accordion. I'm back on home soil now so apologies for making you think that this travel ode type of writing may be taking you to far off corners of the earth. Really I was just alone and a long way from home staring at the ceiling.

1

Another photograph taken earlier in my life in the back garden of our family home on the Rough Hills Estate, Wolverhampton aged about two and also in a pedal car with a toy vehicle in hand and my face in the steering wheel. Hand painted on the side is 'Robie'. It wasn't me that had painted it and one can only assume it was my dad.

Wee Robie ©

2009

Wee Robie fell off a wall
off a wall in Gt Yarmouth,
Wee Robie still has a scar
has a scar on his forehead.

He remembers the trolley in the hospital
and the rubber doors he was pushed through.
Wee Robie what does he do?
his childhood he always goes back to.

Wee Robie still has a scar,
and not the pedal car he had for Christmas.

Looking back on former times and places regardless of being my home town or another has always been an interest of mine. I admire architecture of a previous age albeit in towns that are struggling to survive. People's choices of where and how to shop have made a great impact on the main shopping street in many of our towns and cities.

Former times of our parents and grandparents and earlier have moulded and shaped the area where we were to grow. Mine, as mentioned was on the Rough Hills, a new estate built in the early 1950's which was known for having small coal mines. We lived next door to the Naylor's, near to the Ruscoe's and the Brennan's. Mom became lifetime friends with Mrs Naylor, Dalgleish and Wright. The Parkes's and the Hodson's moved into the close opposite just to name a few. Some became that close that I grew up calling them Auntie's.

Eileen, Dorothy, Connie and Mag
all new families in Rough Hills they were,
a foursome, young mum, neighbour and friend
they trust, they lend and depend

4

I am the middle of three brothers with Gareth being three years older and Stuart eight years younger I was the only one that took to playing football with Gareth being more mechanically minded. Stuart is honest and hard working with a 'always ready to help' approach to life and for a few years in the 1980's we were all Fork Lift Truck Fitters at the same company. Looking back they were really good days and friends were made once again from working side by side on the shop-floor.

The marathon boom was about to take off and many of us were hitting the roads in preparation. I most probably set the ball rolling with my running to work and back so I shall take the credit or blame. A great time for our family was when my brothers and I all ran in the Wolverhampton Marathon in 1985.

Stuart, Robbie and Gareth,
Christmas mid 1960's

"I am me and not another
A husband and son,
a father and brother"

'Wee Robie still has a scar', yes I have a few from my younger days and only a week ago, at the time of writing, my mother said that we were lucky to be living so close to the Royal Hospital!

The Royal Hospital closed and accident and emergency patients have to go to New Cross instead of 'my hospital' further away from our house therefore luck must have been on my side.

To get to town was along Steelhouse Lane, All Saints joining with the Bilston Road at the Horse and Jockey island. All Saints is where my mother was born, where the Church, infant and junior schools were that educated us and a generation before.

All Saints, 2014

"Owen's of All Saints
kicked a casey
(name for an old fashioned ball)
In the playground
against the school wall "

Owen's of All Saints ©

2013

Owen's of All Saints
Kicked a casey
(name for an old fashioned ball)
In the playground
Against the school wall

The streets of All Saints
And Steelhouse Lane
Eagle Street
Whence the Owen's came

Owen's of All Saints
Played their sport
Punched and kicked it
Batted and caught

In their uniforms
And in their teams
Owen's held their own
It's in their genes

9

Owen's of All Saints
In forces for war's of this world
Looking smart in their uniform
Man and girl

And upon a pitch
There is a descendant of
An Owen of All Saints
Me, a poetic artist
What a picture it paints!

Ode related to poem; I Never Knew Him as Grandad.
Benjamin Owen who played in goal for Merthyr Tydfil
before the First World War.

My branch of Owen's from All Saints are known for
having a sporting interest, representing the school of
that name and being in forces and the Special Police
during both the first and second world wars. One was
a senior member of Popski's Private Army, a Special
Force in the Middle East and an aunt was a Spotter
attached to the guns of the ATS.

My mother, born an Owen was also in the ATS and
suffered injuries in an accident whilst serving in Egypt
and was transferred to England on a hospital ship that
she recollects being the El Nil. It was in Aldershot
Military Hospital where she met my dad, a Scotsman
who was also a patient after suffering a motorcycle
accident whilst also in the army.

Ladybank in Fife these days is around 330 miles away
and over a 5 hour drive and is where my dad was
from. I know that for a fact as I have drove it myself
many times in recent years. In Fife you are not too far

away from the East Neuk that's well known for their fishing villages such as Pittenweem and Anstruther. Not only there as St Andrews, an ancestral home of ours, also had a Fisher Quarter. It goes without saying that all Fifer's will know a good piece of fish.

Upon mom introducing dad to her parents, at mealtime, she was shocked to hear him say something like, "that fish was nae caught yesterday, or the day before, or the day before that".

As mentioned they had met whilst in Aldershot Military Hospital. We weren't war babies so to speak but born within the five to ten year period after the Second World War when Great Britain was getting back on its feet. Housing development was needed and the new builds such as the Rough Hills Estate came from there on.

Brown Tanned Arms ©

2006

I remember the rolled up sleeves,
And the brown tanned arms.
The second shirt button that was always undone,
Leaving a tan so dark from the ray of the sun.

When you took off your shirt
you showed lily-white skin,
You laughed from the heart,
You laughed from within.

With your forehead pronouncing
What's more to be said?
Your hair was swept back
Beyond your balding tanned head.
Overalls and a garage and your oily grubby face,
This memory of you I could never replace.

And I still see you laughing
and hear you telling a little white lie,
You were always exaggerating,
We let your romancing pass by.

13

I hear that old Scottish drawl,
The simplified reason of the old Scottish call.

I still look for you to share
a Christmas dinnertime pint of beer,
And again when I'm wishing a Happy New Year.

The sandcastles you built on the beach still stand,
That you made for your sons
with a hard working hand,
The tide may have came and washed them away,
But to me they are still there today.

Dad, my drawing of him
leaning on the wing of a car in a scrapyard on
Steelhouse Lane.

He was a work orientated man, friends with the
Piddock family on Cheviot Road
and Harris's on Rough Hills Close and Jim Dalgliesh
from Dumfries.

That 'old Scottish drawl', although myself being born in Wolverhampton it seems natural for me to hear that accent as it is the the voice that I became accustomed to when a child on the Rough Hills. In recent years I have spent plenty of time in Fife where his voice lingers in the air.

Dad's immediate living Bennet relations had long since left Scotland and were in Suffolk, Louisiana in the USA and another in Toronto, Canada. More research of mine found we had a Bennet further north to us and in Australia.

As far back as I can recall we welcomed the arrival of letters from Louisiana enclosed with genuine heartfelt love for our family.

Letters From Louisiana ©

2014

It's not hard to recall
the time when I was small
a birthday or Christmas card,
now we have e-mails, messages
and texts, wonder what's coming next?

Now and then I draw
on two score years and more before,
when the Postman gave the only
news we were waiting for.

When a letter from Louisiana came
sent with love and signed it with their name,
a letter from Louisiana came
sent with love and could have came,
from far as up in heaven there above,

When a letter from Louisiana did arrive
felt good in Wolverhampton to be alive,
letters from Louisiana when I was a boy
they gave me special moments, so much joy

Thanks Joan and Floyd

Although not having Dad's family living close, the occasional drive was made to Risby, near to the historical market town of Bury St Edmunds in Suffolk. Mom's family were never too far away to visit and cousins were often being introduced.

I wrote with careful consideration of the two people I consider of being my Wolverhampton Grandparents.

My brothers and myself loved them wholeheartedly. Sad circumstances concerning our maternal Grandmother but love overcome of which we are thankful. Sarah Ann, died within weeks of our mother's birth.

On another note, on the first day of September 2013, at the time of writing, the sky was a colourful delight. Coincidently it was also noticed by a cousin of mine.

SARAH ANN AND THE
SEPTEMBER SKY ©

2013

September sky
Striking it is, oh why?
As I try to write of, Sarah Ann

A Sunday light blue
And I'm writing of you
A Sunday light blue, Sarah Ann, I can see
As the evening draws in, gradually

Fifty nine summers so far
Fifty nine summers
None shared with Sarah Ann
My maternal Gran, Sarah Ann

A father of two I became
Feels good to tell you and write your name
Bloodline, from the same
Aren't we Sarah Ann?

Fifty nine summers
Fifty nine summers, Sarah Ann, I have had
Four children call me Grandad
And for your daughter, my mother, I am glad
Sarah Ann, your story is sad

Motherhood, a premature end
Your six children couldn't comprehend
From newborn up to aged eleven
Asking why, their mother, had to go to heaven?

A mother of three boys, your baby daughter became
Feels good to tell you and write your name
Into my mind you came
My maternal Gran, Sarah Ann

We missed you Sarah Ann
In the passing of time
Now, Sarah Ann
You are sharing these minutes of mine

September sky
Amazing, why oh why?
As the sky is red Sarah Ann
And now, a Sunday dark blue

A Sunday dark blue
As I'm writing of you
A Sunday dark blue, Sarah Ann I have said
Is it you in that September sky, that September red?

That September red, Sarah Ann I have said
If true, Sarah Ann, if true
My fifty ninth summer
... Then I've shared this summer with you!

I Never Knew Him as Grandad ©

2005

I never knew him as grandad
I loved him, who stood in his place,
I grew up without understanding
Not thinking to picture his face.

In a time of worries and troubles
An age of conflict and war,
Who is the man in the photo?
To my thoughts I open the door.

His regiment was the 4TH Lincoln's
Held captive but made his escape,
Wounded by a bullet in a shoulder
Desperate and in poor shape.

The battlefield he crawled for four days
Drinking water from bottles of dead,
French Officers saw movement in a body
Injured by bullets of lead.

Discharged in 1918
In his regiment he could no longer be,
He was no longer physically able
A young man of just twenty-three.

He lived on to be forty-one
But pneumonia set in and he died,
I never knew him as grandad
Then inside a part of me cried.

Mom's aunt and uncle became her adopted parents
and the grandparents that we loved and adored.

A TRIBUTE TO NAN
AND GRANDAD ©

1991

My Grandad was a quiet man
But still liked family around.
While Nan sat there talking
He'd hardly say a sound.
Sitting in his armchair
Hearing others talk,
Never ever offending
Often liked to walk.
I can see him in his suit and tie
Looking neat and smart,
My Grandad was a quiet man
With the biggest kindest heart.

My Nan she always told stories
Of the old days and years gone by,
She must have been a young rascal
I can tell by that look in her eye.
The cheekiest grin on a lady
Will never be seen no more,
I'm sure up in heaven God's smiling
Since Jane Rowley has passed through his door.

We have a picture of my Grandad taken looking immaculate as usual in Bridgnorth. He was a Rowley, an excellent footballer himself by all accounts, and a name of distinction in the football world due to his cousins. This young newly married man and his wife were my mothers aunt and uncle and adopted her as a baby and were also from the All Saints area of Wolverhampton. I can recall being so proud of him coming to see me play football in Bushbury only to suffer a hammering of a defeat.

Since 1998, I have got to know Ian Crichton who is associated with Wolverhampton Schools Football. He produces programmes for the District Fixtures and Arthur and Jack Rowley, my Grandads cousins are often mentioned. The Rowley name always reaches home.

The Rowley Name ©

2007

In my line is the Rowley name,
Goal scoring records and football fame.
War torn interrupted professional careers,
Once more I reflect on bygone years.
My Grandad was a Rowley too,
Been paid to play if he wanted to.
But Nan she always knew the score,
Keep the bad wolf from our door.
A cartilage injury I also heard,
Was that the reason and not Nan's strong word.
So cousin George chose not to play the game,
Jack and Arthur progressed to football fame.
When he was about age sixty-seven,
I would then be around eleven.
We were kicking a ball on a Somerset beach,
My modern skills I tried to teach.
But he had such a delicate touch,
That impressed I can't describe how much.
I forgot my Grandad was a Rowley too,
Been paid to play if he wanted to.

I noticed how soon he selected his pass,
On a Somerset beach not on a field of grass.
One day when I was just sixteen,
I played right back in a pro-Youth Team.
He came to Stafford to see me play,
I remember it well, except the score that day.
Come the time about twenty-two,
I knew it all like young men do.
He was watching me play there on the line,
I think that day I was number nine.
I can't recall another game,
After that match that my Grandad came.
I've never forgot he was a Rowley too,
Been paid to play if he wanted to.
Although time fades and less they preach,
I saw it all on a Somerset beach.
Goal scoring records and football fame.
The highly reputable Rowley name.

Major Street 2013

"seems yesterday my first school day
up Major Street
past the twin peaked wall at Bayliss's,
Bayliss Jones Bayliss's"

I was soon following my elder brother to All Saints Junior School and I can still recall my first day as mother and I walked along Major Street. I found the school building tall and daunting and when asked if I had enjoyed being there I replied "yes, but I didn't want to come tomorrow."

In a couple of years I was to be one of the dancers around the Maypole and an attendant to the May Queen. Years later I was to be the Grandfather of a baby girl born on the first of May.

Eagle Street, 2014

"run once more
on Dixon Street once more,
down Dixon Street up Major Street
once more

Cable Street and Eagle Street
with youngsters feet once more"

Mom was born just over the road from All Saints Church in Eagle Street and many a relation before me had also attended and played for the school football team. She was later to be a Barmaid in the Summer House nearby and I can recall running from town to show her my medal after becoming the 1965 Cross Country Champion of Staffordshire to retain it the year later again at Aldersley Stadium.

Steelhouse Lane, 2013

"was it Marandola's doors that I recall?
the cinder wall seemed trait and tall
near the Summerhouse
on Steelhouse Lane, All Saints
where a register had my name.

how strange, a register had my name?"

Shadow of All Saints ©

2014

Names of roads and lanes
footpaths on streets,
where my childhood feet
once went and came

Even though it's nae the coast
o my ancestral Fife,
here are memories
my early All Saints life

Even though I'm nae
aside the sparkling Tay,
here are memories
until whatever day named my last day

Hear my fathers Scottish drawl
calling me 'tae to cam hame for tea',
see my mothers smiling face
outside of school at my All Saints,
near the street where she was born

in the shadow,
near to a shadow of All Saints

Buildings gone
school children have moved on,
husbands, wives, partners, careers
leaving their childhood years

Where are the voices?
the hundred workers from the factories
Where are the songs?
The melodies that springs memories

Thank The Lord
I hear them now and then
Where are the girls and boys?
That matured and came women and men

I saw them on number thirty bus
swaying down Steelhouse Lane,
to town they went
and back they came

Even though it's nae the coast
o my ancestral Fife,
here are memories
my early All Saints life

Even though I'm nae
aside the sparkling Tay,
here are memories
until whatever day named my last day

In the shadow,
warm it is the shadow,
in the shadow of All Saints

All Saints Church, 2014

"see my mothers smiling face
outside of school at my All Saints,
near the street where she was born
in the shadow,
near to a shadow of All Saints"

A Little Boys Prayer ©

2014

This was the church
that first heard my prayer,
a little boys prayer

this was the church
that since that day
I see churches everywhere

this was the church
that blessed marriage
of kin and birth,

this was the church
that saw an imaginative lad
see the good and not the bad

this was the church
that welcomed me so
and watched me grow

this was the church
that saw me fly away
like a bird

this was the church
where my first prayer,
a little boys prayer
was heard

All Saints Church, 2014

"This was the church
that first heard my prayer,
a little boys prayer"

Here I was one late winters morning in 2014 standing in All Saints Road rekindling feelings of being at this school building until aged 11. Within a few months I was to celebrate my 60th year so there was plenty to recall and I am sure that most has been forgotten.

Behind where I was standing was an all-weather sports pitch which occupies the land which once was St Joseph's Catholic School. I took photographs of the building of All Saints School and Church which are now used for other purposes. The Church of England School opened in 1894 and closed in the 1990's. Upon researching the history of both church and school, I was pleasantly surprised to find that the church is faced with pinkish Codsall sandstone blocks and Staffordshire terracotta tiles on the pitched roof. Codsall in Staffordshire is now where I live which married my present to my past.

I stood by the perimeter fence of the school, looking up at windows where my childhood eyes would have looked out of many times.

A SEA of
ALL SAINTS MEMORIES ©
2014

Staring at the brickwork
from my viewpoint by the railings,
my mind goes drifting and sailing
on a sea of a memories

Staring at a window where,
I would have stared through a window there,
at this viewpoint where
I'm standing by the railings

Climbed stairs in that building
and walked through many a classroom door,
in amongst chattering children
fifty and five more years before

The bell did ring for playtime
playtime and dinner time,
around the building the bell did chime
again did ring at home time

Lunchtime meals were eaten
in the dinner hall next door,
six or eight children at a long table
could have been a couple more

Watching and playing Rounders
on a painted pitch on the playground,
the feeling's now coming rushing
bat and ball, the smack, the sound

The pole went up in the playground
in the Springtime month of May,
young me on a photograph
with the May Queen, back in the day

Parents and family came
chairs were positioned in regimental line
to watch the Morris Dancing Team
sticks and bells were heard in time

On special days in All Saints Church
a visit was paid from each class,
I remember these days so well
when I'm close and occasionally I pass

Staring at the brickwork
from my viewpoint by the railings,
my mind still drifting and sailing
on a sea of a memories

It must now be home time
or into that sea this man has fell,
for I imagine seeing a pupil,
running and ringing the bell

...from my viewpoint by the railings.

"A sea of All Saints memories,
from that viewpoint by the railings"

Fifty and more years later from being in my first school
playground I was to stop by again to take a few more
pictures of All Saints Church. I ventured a little bit
further this time and went on to the car park of the old
school building. My mind was active in remembering
when this was our playground.

I looked up the side of the school building and
followed the instruction of No Entry but admittedly
tempted to take a walk to the back of the school to see
the other playground. I could see the top corner where
chairs were placed in line for the spectators coming
for the Morris Dancing.

There would have been many little feet of my mom's
side of the family running around also well before my
time. I imagined them all and seeing the Church where
weddings and christenings have taken place.

When a former fellow pupil saw my picture of the
playground he reminded me of the exact place that
some 55 years ago we sat holding our flower pole
garlands for the May Queen. It had made him a bit
tearful. We have that picture in the family. I searched

for that and other old school photographs to make comparisons. Not only has the school and playground changed but the Dinner Hall has gone and is now a garden and the church is a community centre. Trees were also young and like me yet to mature.

It was a peaceful ten minutes standing somewhere where I had not done so for fifty years. 'A man of thought but sometimes thoughtless' browsing around, his childhood playground.

MY CHILDHOOD
PLAYGROUND ©

2014

Had a browse around
my childhood playground,
I couldn't hear the same sound
of my childhood playground

This quiet June Sunday afternoon
years pass too soon,
time flies too fast
make your memories last

White shirts
short trousers of grey,
we'd run around that way
back in my day

Laughing and playing around
my childhood playground,
I found I was at peace with the sound
here, on the car park, my childhood playground

All Saints School, 2014.
Once was my childhood playground.

*"I couldn't hear the same sound
of my childhood playground,
this quiet June Sunday afternoon
years pass too soon"*

I Only Knew Him by Name ©

2014

I had a conversation by
a war memorial today,
I only knew him by name
peace in mind then came,
this speechless conversation
with someone's family loved one,
their fallen relation,
I only knew him by name
rest in peace, brave sir once again

All Saints Church, 2014

War Memorials, they always attract my attention, in Wolverhampton, my ancestral Scotland or elsewhere. I recognise surnames that I know of in Wolverhampton and wonder if they are a relative of those. I take a photo to find that I have taken one before of the same memorial. In Scotland I look for Kennedy and Bennet with one 't' at the end. No matter where I may be, I always engage in their difficult time.

I've walked alone for many miles and turned a corner to see a War Memorial in a Village or Town that I have never been to. I change my thoughts instantly and read names of those who have given their all.

No matter what time of night or day or wherever you may be when you read the above, I write it at almost 10.30pm in the almost darkness of my back garden.

Next morning I had a nostalgic hour at All Saints Church in Wolverhampton. I had completed my poem 'I Only Knew Him by Name' and wanted a War Memorial or Plaque to be pictured. My thoughts were to bring my past into present by finding if All Saints Church had anything on display. Here I was to be

shown around the church by the Caretaker Phil
Collins and he allowed me to take a few pictures and
display If I wish to of the war plaque and other scenes.
I got the impression that he was pleased to have me as
a visitor albeit uninvited.

At first I was thinking that I may be out of luck as the
church was locked. It now doubles as a community
centre. I pressed the buzzer at the Child Care in the
Community part of the church. Although the young
lady was pleased that I had an interest she could not
answer my question. I also had no joy in my old school
building where she directed me.

Upon returning to my car on All Saints Road I noticed
two men with clipboards making notes of the church.
There was no joy there either as they appeared to be
pointing out maintenance work.

As I was about to give in and get in my car I noticed a
fellow wearing an identification tag. He soon assisted
with my task and called the Caretaker. I found that this
was Phil Collins and thoroughly knowledgeable on the
church. His enthusiasm shone through as he gave me

chapter and verse of the changes and what problems they have had to overcome.

Without doubt I can say that my mind was once again taken back to over half a century. My eyes were everywhere as I tried to listen intently to what Phil was telling me. There was even forgotten pictures on the wall of Jesus that I recognised in detail. It really is amazing what the memory stores to release whenever the time comes. I would be a boy aged between 5 and 10 years gazing at those framed pictures on the wall.

Back in the early sixties I became a football mad youngster, always down the fields at the bottom of our road with my mates. We would be kicking the ball about for hours on end. Playing for the love of the game and before I could understand the rules, I was selected for the football team. I can recall the feel of the kit and the bag I was given and that some shirts were faded more than others. The number 8 was a beauty, colours bold and smart. I had shirt number 7 and to describe it has been around the block and back would be an understatement.

Well I was in the team and football was getting a grip into my life and here are my thoughts in 2006.

Bennett You're Offside ©

2006

When first I kicked a ball,
I was very small,
Selected to play upon the wing.

I had a wee bit of pace,
An average kind of face,
From the bye line I made the ball ping.

I thought that I was in heaven,
When he gave me the shirt number seven.
Nothing that day could dent my pride,
They called me Bennett You're Offside.

Just a wee lad of nine,
Following instructions to hug the line.
I remember I scored a goal that day,
A life in the game I was well on my way.

I lay in a hospital bed,
With blood oozing from a wound in my head.
A few operations I've had to have done,
To play the game for fun.

In the box I was lethal and fast
I've been the unused sub,
Took the card around the pub
I've been off work with a plaster cast.

I've seen tantrums and fights,
Played under floodlights,
A tackle or two was late.
I've got arthritic dodgy knees
Ignored 'don't play again please'
But football was my fate.

I've taken the early bath,
He wasn't really hurt he was having a laugh.
I've played in a men's team
Just turning fifteen,
The dressing room humour was fun.
Bowling green pitches butterfly stitches,
Played in the same team as my son.

Oh the game of football
Leads you a merry dance,
Dislocations and scars
Hit the net and crossbars,
And I've missed the easy chance.

Father time slowed down my tricks,
So I called it a day aged about forty-six.
And now over fifty I recall it all,
The ups and downs in the life of football.

To some it is only a game,
As I'm setting off to a match in the rain.
Then a photo in a frame catches my eye,
And many a season has passed on by.
Chalked on the well faded brown leather ball,

Is the year of 1963.
In the front row is Bennett you're offside,
That's what they were shouting at me.

Bennett You're Offside

I have mentioned earlier of Benjamin James Owen (poem I Never Knew Him as Grandad) playing in goal for Methyr Tydfil. Close to Methyr Tydfil in Wales at a nearby village, an eventful dark day is set in my mind. At 9.15am on Friday 21st October 1966 the Aberfan Disaster happened and shall never be forgot. Fog was lying as a coal slag waste tip slid down the mountainside into the Welsh village swallowing up a farm cottage, Pantglas Junior School and nearby houses. A total of 144 people lost their life of which 116 were pupils of the school.

Unbelievable scenes were shown endlessly on the Rediffusion TV that we paid an agreed rental fee for. The collector was Mrs Porter from Rooker Avenue mother of cyclist Hugh Porter MBE, who now has the entrance drive named after him at Aldersley Leisure Village.

The Aberfan Disaster was to add to another shocking event 3 years earlier in 1963 when President Kennedy was assassinated in Dallas. I can recall playing a Marmite Sandwich game of being squashed in between chair and settee cushions with Brian Ruscoe from 2 doors down. The door opened and mom walked in to break the news to us.

We were innocent with our thinking and bad news did not come into our world. Whatever we heard on the news appeared to be elsewhere.

The endless evenings before home entertainment, other than black and white television, were spent out in the street. It would have dropped dark and no doubting that we would have had the orders of "don't go away from the house".

The starry sky was the obvious to be looking at and the Plough was the favourite. We found, disagreed and changed our minds to which one was the North Star.

Sorting Out The Stars ©

2011

Kids upon a Rough Hills curb
sorting out the stars,
tucking in our toes
because of passing cars

Oh, to be a kid again
childhood has closed the door,
oh, to be a kid again
a kid again once more

Sorting out the stars
and searching for the Plough,
I become that kid again
when I'm looking for it now

No matter where I am on Earth
to my childhood, this is how,
I scrutinise a starry sky
and like a kid I find the Plough

When I find the Plough
I am in a Rough Hills night,
there upon a council curb
tucking my toes in tight

Our family doctor was on Snow Hill, either a long walk or a bus ride to town. I can recall the side door entrance and chairs in the narrow waiting room. We would be seen by Dr Wallace, a man who appeared to gain immediate respect or a lady Dr Young. When we were really ill we had the house calls after the surgery had closed and to have Dr Wallace in the confine of our home was indescribable. I always felt a sigh of relief whenever he left the house and confirmed that I was really ill, advising my mother that I should have some time away from school.

In later years and Dr Wallace now not in the practice, the surgery moved to a new building in Blakenhall, near to the Dudley Road. In later years my visits were always sport related and I sensed an unwelcome tone when I heard, "oh, it's Bennett the footballer".

Dr Wallace on Snow Hill ©

2014

Whenever I felt ill,
my mother could always tell,
or if I needed
medical attention as well

Like seven days after
hospital treatment,
and a prescription
for ointment or a pill,
Mom would take me to my Doctor,
Dr Wallace on Snow Hill

I can remember the waiting room,
seats either side,
no where to scramble or scrawl
for this wee laddie to hide

We waited for my name to be called
Dr Wallace would be there in his chair,
I couldn't misbehave in front of Dr Wallace
no, this wee laddie wouldn't dare

Any roads, I wasn't well,
if I was kidding Dr Wallace could tell,
even now I get that feeling still
of my Doctor,
Dr Wallace on Snow Hill

I once wrote of Thomas Joseph Harris aged 16 who was the first to lose his life in building the Forth Bridge in 1883. This is another Harris but this time from Wolverhampton who I have mentioned in a childhood memory poem of mine.

Douglas Harris's parents were originally from London and he was born in 1898 and according to the 1901 and 1911 census's they lived on Penn Road and Lea Road.

The Harris Sculpture by Robert Jackson Emerson (1878-1944)

It was in St Peter's Gardens that we met for our away games when playing for All Saints Junior School.

Douglas Morris Harris,
St Peters

"There I noticed the bust of a Sailor
and I read of his bravery
on loan to the Floandi
torpedoed in the Adriatic Sea"

Douglas Morris Harris Born in Penn ©

2014

Teacher called me one day
to attend an important induction
meet at St Peter's Gardens, Saturday morning
Mr Lancaster's instruction

I'd made All Saints football team
Dot and Jock's laddie well under eleven
a khaki army kit-bag I carried
containing shirt number seven

It was a grand old morning in Summer
flowers I was a counting
bedding plants were a blooming
and admiring the Horsman Fountain

There I noticed the bust of a Sailor
and I read of his bravery
on loan to the Floandi
torpedoed in the Adriatic Sea

71

Amidst this fearful attack
Douglas Morris Harris born in Penn
continued to call for assistance
to the Floandi and all her men

Douglas refused to leave his duty
this Wireless Operator's life was lost
Just paying my respect for Douglas
respect, how much does it cost?

In nineteen seventeen
one night in the month of May
Lest we forget Douglas Harris
thank you, is all I can say

I look back on that football induction
Dot and Jock's laddie in nineteen sixty three
this Able Seaman gave a lesson
of notable people in Wolverhampton history

Dixon Street Playing Fields looking to the Monkey House.

It was this pitch that I had my first game of organised football.

"It was raining
I was told
could have been wet
could have been cold"

A Boy, alone, on a Wet, Cold Field in Parkfields ©

2005

It was raining
I was told
could have been wet
could have been cold

could have been you
on that field
all alone
could have been you
200 yards from home

could have been him
could have been her
could have been someone
with a huge transfer

could have been you
or any other
but it was me
seen by my mother

walking to Darby's in Dixon Street
200 yards from home
it was me on that field
all alone

with a ball at my feet
waiting for a mate
was I early I ask?
or is he too late?

it was true,
my mother she told
me, about eleven years old

she was walking back from Darby's
and she saw me
in the wet and the cold

nineteen sixty's me
in the rain and the sleet
with a ball at my feet

a boy, alone,
on a wet cold field in Parkfields

Dixon Street playing fields in Parkfields,
Wolverhampton in the 1960's. Plenty of lads from the
Rough Hills Estate and All Saints would congregate
and play a match for hours on end. Far too many for a
11 x side game. If you were there you joined in and
played. Quite often it was 10 goals for half-time and
twenty the winner but come Sunday it was a monster
of match. We kicked off in the morning and resumed
after dinner in the afternoon. The pitch was probably
as wide as it was long. The one touchline was the path
that went from Dixon St to Kent Road and Pond Lane.
At about mid-day when the Monkey House pub
opened blokes would pass by on their way for a pint
sometimes stopping for a while to see our game.

Cheviot Road, sometime in the 1970's

"we played curb with the ball
tick in the street
hop scotch on the slabs
summer holidays,
rock pools and crabs"

A ROUGH HILLS KID ©

2008

Only a Rough Hills kid
can't recall any harm that I did
an ordinary lad from a Wolverhampton estate
in streets and fields, footballing mates

an ordinary Rough Hills kid
not far from the Tavern and Monkey I lived
we played curb with the ball
tick in the street
hop scotch on the slabs
summer holidays, rock pools and crabs

rattle, tat, tat when we kicked the can
we kicked the can then ran,
knocking marbles out of the ring
by the railway bridge, 'Doog is King'

towpath led us to another world
canal and factory smell
peacefulness and noise
growing up days for us girls and boys

one hot summer the field caught fire
honest truth, not known as a liar
fire engines with sirens arrived
boys on the field survived

'to spread our wings and fly,
expand our wings and fly, fly, fly'

we were never really in danger
safe was this Rough Hills Ranger!
to live to tell the story
more ordinary than battles and glory

Just an ordinary Rough Hills kid
can't recall any harm that I did
an ordinary lad from a Wolverhampton estate
in streets and fields, footballing mates

The Rough Hills Tavern sign on Rooker Avenue

"an ordinary Rough Hills kid
not far from the Tavern
and Monkey I lived"

I was once in conversation with someone and mentioned this poem. He knew Dixon Street playing fields very well. He played for Coseley Amateurs and recalled the old tin huts that were so called changing rooms. One game had to be held up as another path ran diagonally across the pitch and a woman was walking to Pond Lane with her shopping.

The playing field at the time of writing is being redeveloped and levelled to make another flat pitch and the Monkey House is boarded-up. Whenever I drive by I can still feel the excitement. I recall that time in my life when those games meant so much to me and I'm sure that there are others who feel the same way.

Dixon Street, 2011

"Were you one of the thirty?
Were you one of the bunch,
Dixon Street on a Sunday,
second-half played after lunch"

Were You One of The Thirty Who Played In The Dixon St Game? ©

2008

My world was down the road from me
At the bottom of our street,
On Sunday and every summer night
The lads from the estate would meet.

Were you one of the thirty?
Were you one of the bunch,
Dixon Street on a Sunday
Second-half played after lunch.

By the Monkey House in the sixties
Disputing a goal or not,
Fallouts were often forgotten
Jumpers for goal posts was what we got.

Were you one of the thirty?
Slide tackling and getting dirty,

I invite you to enter your name
If you played in the Dixon Street game.

The idea of writing the poem came from being invited to Goodyear's Social Club for Roger Bull. Not wanting to go into detail at this moment, it was nice to be remembered and contacted. There were lads there I hadn't seen for over 20 years and we were soon talking about the football matches on Dixon Street.

For many years I have written poems about the old days. I realized that there were many like me who knew we had something special in the playing fields at Dixon Street.

It played on my mind for a while and I knew that I should write a poem about 'our' field. I was down there one Sunday (March 2009) watching 2 games of football. Whilst there I heard a motorbike coming out of Cheviot Road. I instinctively looked over to see if it was my elder brother. That's inside of my mind because it's what I used to do when I was a teenager playing down the fields.

For a few hours my thoughts were all over the place seeing how it had changed. Trees and bushes around the field with a perimeter path. The MEB offices had gone, so had the old tin sheds with the fence behind and the Monkey House was boarded up. The council are working hard levelling the ground for new football pitches and there is in now a park for youngsters. So there will be football and memories for other generations to come.

On a week day dinnertime workers would be over the field playing a game of football. On the odd occasion they would be one short and I could 'get a game'. Also on a Thursday afternoon when walking home from school a match would be on for the shop workers. At that time Thursday was half day closing and there was a football league for all who were unable to play on Saturday.

After a few years of playing games amongst ourselves we decided to get opposition from lads from other areas. We needed a name and chose Rough Hills Rangers. This was a time before youth football leagues and no adults shown interest except Peter Morton's dad Bill. So we had a team and an adopted manager but who chose whom? This proved to be fine except we did not have a regular goalkeeper until about 1966–67 when 'Hoddy' came to the estate. Barry Hodson, a proper goalie, not forgetting young Malcolm Hodgkins, moved to the Rough Hills from Eastfield and was immediately given the number one slot.

It was interesting to see the names start appearing in my Guest Book and I can't help wondering who is going to be next?

The first Guest Book message from Simon Askey;
I was one of the thirty but five years later. Also played for Park Hall juniors in 73 on pitch by The Monkey. Played for Park Hall Juniors on the pitch by the Monkey.
All Saints Sports Day,winning the 60 mtr sack race.
Many happy memories playing football and cricket down the field.
Thanks for the memories., Simon

Guest Book message From John Meese;
Joined 67-68 season,probably the youngest of the 30,
never threatened,always encouraged,what lovely
memories and happy days. The Browns, Big Chris,
Weave, Clampy, Kiddle, Pyder,Bully,Benny,H,The
Pitts,Billy Walker and all. I remember Rough Hills
Rangers played a friendly at Bantock Park arranged by
Micky Brown. Won 2-0. The opposition wanted to buy
Robbie and Ian Bosworth for 10 shillings. Best mates,
great memories!
Comment by: John Meese

Guest Book message from Dave Brown;
so bennetts into poetry and i guess he's pretty good,he
was'nt a bad footballer especially in the mud . those
good old sunday mornings playing till we dropped
usually finishing off the game around 4 o'clock.
best wishes Dave.

Guest Book message from Barry Hodson;
Hi Robbie told you I know how to get on the page sum
good stuff but I thought I inspired you good luck mate
Comment by: Barry Hodson

Guest Book message from Barry Hodson;
*Thanks for the mention about being a real goalie good
for the ego.*
Comment by: Barry Hodson

Guest Book Message from the Author;
*They say that a goalie has to be daft, he has to be daft
and has to be saft, Well there's no one dafter than
Hoddy, no one safter than Hoddy. Have I told you they
have to be brave, occasionally be able to make a great
save? Hoddy was brave and could make a great save,
that's all that I want you to know. But I must be daft
and I must be saft, to blow up his dam blasted ego!*
Comment by: Robbie

Guest Book Message
*I loved that one about the thirty Robbie and your
comments after about it now.*
Comment by: rick

Guest Book Message;
*Just discovered your site while doing some family
research. Ex-Cheviot Road and All Saints school.
Football – Dixon Street or Rooker Avenue/Lawn Road.
Anyone remember Glynmar FC or Bridge Sports*

(1967+)? Speedway at Monmore Green in the 60's. Trainspotting (steam) by the 'cut' or by the bridge near Monmore Green stadium in the late 50's. The Rooker Avenue shops. The no. 30 bus. Thanks for the Rough Hills photos and memories, Robbie. Keep up the good work.
Comment by: Derek Mills

So the 'Thirty' poem about lads from Rough Hills, Parkfields and All Saints is alive and kicking, some of our 'Thirty' and of another. Prompted by Roger Bull who lived further a field near to Snow Hill.

Every summer we looked forward to the Home Internationals. The British Home Championship, the oldest international football tournament which was abolished in 1983-84 after a hundred years with Northern Ireland being the last champions.

I had a foot in both camps having dual English and Scottish parents and all teams in those days appear to have a great or two. Personally I have always liked to have a sprinkle of Scottish grit in football teams and some First Division sides had one as a captain. There is also great tradition with a Scotsman in the managerial position.

Obviously more of the Scottish players in the 1960's were known to me than to my mates. I can recall one day when in a friends house watching England and Scotland at Wembley. I was surprised to find that my mate did not know a certain player. I was to sing his praises for the next 10 minutes prior to kick off for him to have a torrid opening to the game. This was one of my first experiences of the Scottish pride of my family side being hurt as I had to defend his talent.

Incidentally, I was to be in a club in St Andrews, Fife in Summer of 2013 to watch on television the England versus Scotland fixture at Wembley. It was a great feeling after all these years to be in Scotland at the time especially in an ancestral home of St Andrews. From the club window I could see the harbour and the birthplace of my Great Grandmother. For the record the game was drawn and there are calls to revive the match.

St Andrews, Fife, Scotland,
an ancestral home

"Then I thought I heard a whistle
I turned and saw a thistle,
blowing in the breeze not far away"

I Thought I Heard a Whistle ©

2009

Walking down Wembley Way,
With a letter from Alf picking us to play.
All those bobbing heads and rattles in hand
Seen it on the telly and listened to the marching band

Possibly 12 years old,
Dreaming of wearing the shirt of gold.
Mates on Dixon Street with a ball
Were all awaiting an international call

Then I thought I heard a whistle
I turned and saw a thistle,
Blowing in the breeze not far away.

We all stood around picking a side
An important decision the result relied,
For club and country when the game does start
Give it all and follow your heart.

Then I thought I heard a whistle
I turned and saw a thistle,
Blowing in the breeze not far away.

Did anyone hear a whistle?
I thought I saw a thistle,
We chose our position and then kicked off to play
Then one day the thistle came to stay.

The gates at the bend of Major Street
and Steelhouse Lane

*"run once more
on Dixon Street once more,
down Dixon Street
up Major Street once more,
down Dixon Street up Major Street
with youngsters feet once more"*

I can't recall the bricklayers building the new houses near to the Monkey House but all of a sudden they were there. That brought new life with youngsters on to the field which spiced up our games of football and cricket.

Mentioning the Monkey House, it appeared to be a good pub with bar and lounge at the front and outdoor and kids room at the back. There were benches in the patio area with a field next door. What more could a young family in the 1960's ask for?

The Monkey House or Moulders Arms, 2013

"The Monkey House
is boarded up and empty
changes are a plenty"

Many years later I would return to the Monkey House with my wife and children for a bonfire. If times were the same and the pub was open, I would have gone there last Bonfire Night and many more before and after.

Socially my growing up area has changed with the closure of not only the Monkey but the Rough Hills Tavern, Silver Birch and Black Horse. At the time of writing the Monkey is the only building still standing. Having mentioned that people must have changed also in not using the establishments.

Nevertheless in our time the amount of lads on the field was expanding and games were becoming a wee bit more serious.

Moulders Arms, 2014

"I say goodbye to Bradley Road
I could cry
for the state of the Moulders,
and the field's not ours no more
weekends, weekdays
after half-past four"

Bradley Road, Over by the Moulders ©

2014

The new build on Bradley Road
over by the Moulders,
more young un's came and rubbed shoulders

over by the Moulders,
The Monkey or The Moulders

Pitt's and Clamp
Brown's and Brace,
new blood on the field
an unfamiliar face,
over by the Moulders

When they built Bradley Road
over by the Moulders,
Keith Passmore played
with the swagger of Best,
new boys came and joined the rest,
in many a kick-about game

over by the Moulders,
The Monkey or The Moulders

Now when I'm by Bradley Road
over by the Moulders,
I often remember those games
and I remember most of their names,
probably more that I need reminding
and someone else I'll be finding from
over by the Moulders

I say goodbye to Bradley Road
I could cry for the state of the Moulders,
and the field's not ours no more
weekends, weekdays after half-past four,

over by the Moulders,
The Monkey or The Moulders

Pitt's and Clamp
Brown's and Brace,
new blood on the field
we have been replaced
over by the Moulders

... the field's not ours no more,

over by the Moulders,
The Monkey or The Moulders

Steelhouse Lane, opposite Cable Street

"along winding Steelhouse Lane,
good for me I thought,
admitting, sometimes
number 30 bus I caught"

Walking to Town ©

2014

Said "goodbye"
to Mom at home in Cheviot Road,
"walking to town,
I'm walking to town"

Said "hi"
to football friends as I
was walking to town,
walking to town

Said "hi"
to my Dad there,
I said "hi"
rubbing shoulders in the Moulders
"Are ye walking tae toon, Robbie?
"Walking tae toon"

We lived not far
from Wolverhampton town,
in a rented council house
that we did not then own

Said "hi"
to once my Grandparents home,
said a nostalgic "hi"
to the corner dwelling,
because I couldn't walk by,
without saying "hi"
as I was walking to town
walking to town

Said "hi"
to the Caledonia guy,
name of his store
I called like many times before

Said "hi"
to the cinder wall still there,
why did my Grandmother care?
that they didn't pull it down
walking to town

Said "hi"
to All Saints Church and School
Said "hi"
to Joey's as well, never failing,
to run my hand along the railing
walking to town

I walked to town quite often
along winding Steelhouse Lane,
good for me I thought,
admitting, sometimes
number 30 bus I caught

Said "hi"
to the Royal Hospital
and Horse and Jockey,
Said "hi"
to Doody's Paper Shop
as I passed them by
as I was walking to town
walking to town

Said "hi"

to Cleveland Road Bus Depot,

soon near Pipers Row,

close enough to town,

one drove in for repair

as I was walking past there

as I was walking to town

walking to town

Said "hi"

did Wolverhampton town to me,

where children were always shouting with glee

"We're Minors of the ABC!

Like My Grandad Before Me I'm Gold, a story ode of football support passed down in a family. I now attend matches with my son and eldest Grandson. Summer 2013 was a special ancestral moment as aged 6 this grandson played on Molineux wearing a Scotland kit.

The poem is also for all supporters who are fans of their home town club. It is tempting when young to want to be connected to a more successful team. This support stays put and you wish and hope that one day your turn will come. If ever you see a game on television and the camera focuses on the old guy when his team who are the underdogs have scored, think of his story and him being there.

It's good to be attending a game with someone else but I often notice elderly fans on their own. There must be an abundance of highs and lows in their time and what a strength to still keep going alone.

All clubs have and need loyal supporters and if it's the team that their Grandad supported then it's definitely in the blood.

LIKE MY GRANDAD BEFORE ME
I'M GOLD ©

2002

Do you have a dream or a memory?

Or have you a story to tell.

My elders speak of The Wanderers,

To me they've no need to sell.

They've seen the old gold

on a green hallowed turf

It was a proud and wonderful sight.

The Molineux roar was heard from afar

On a nostalgic European night.

The boys that reigned in the fifty's,

The promotion of the late sixty's.

The seventy's team had flair,

In the eighty's we were nearly not there.

I've respectfully mentioned no names,

For they gave what they could in Wolves games.

And no I never would hurt,

That pride of wearing a gold shirt.

I'm sure you and I will agree,

I wished that could have been me.

The ninety's we began to look fine,

We unearthed a great number nine.

And we still cheer them on during games,

The old gold runs on through our veins.

As the glory recedes in the shade,

Our time in the shadows we've paid.

Like my Grandad before me I'm gold,

To the red of the north I'm not sold.

We are Wulfrunians,

We are what we are.

Why search for success from afar.

We're out of the darkness

And into the light,

We'll dream of a European night.

And to see the old gold on a green hallowed turf,

Would be a proud and wonderful sight.

Statues around football grounds of great players and managers. Some clubs have them and some don't, but they all have individuals who are the bricks, mortar and fabric of the football club.

I was born within a week of Wolves being crowned First Division Champions for the first time in 1953-54. The plaque on Stan Cullis's statue reads "In this world, you have only one life, and I gave mine to Wolves."

The older generation to mine often speak of the great players who have played for Wolves and I can only respect those opinions that have been passed down. I can recall being taken to Butlers Sports Ground by my uncle to see a cousin and an Owen play against a team of Old Wolves Stars. I was mesmerised by the ability of the veteran players and can only remember the goalkeeper Malcolm Finlayson because of his stature.

Manager of Wolves in the golden years was former player Stan Cullis and he is my reminder of my childhood conversations with my elders and my hand down to my Grandchildren.

"Who is that Grandad?
"It's Stan Cullis boy's, manager in the 1950's when
Wolves were a mighty force".
"Wow! Came the reply.

The Stan Cullis Statue
Molineux Stadium
Produced by Warwickshire based sculpture
James Butler 2003

Stan Cullis Statue at Molineux

"He stands with his hat,
held in his hand,
and there are Wolves shirts
all over the land"

He Stands With His Hat, Held in His Hand ©

2004

When a man becomes a legend
Should we be then beholden?
For he was a fearless fellow
And he made Wolves history golden.
This brave heart man from Ellesmere Port
Brought back honour to the shirt,
He wore Gold colours and gave them pride
With blood, soaked sweat and dirt.

For him they would not dare to hide
When chose to play in his great side.
His final walk out of the managers door
Was in the year of sixty-four.
By then he had given them glory
He left behind a story.
And a football birth to famous names
The floodlit nights and memorable games.
Now by him all legends are measured
At Molineux his days are treasured.

He stands with his hat, held in his hand
And there are Wolves shirts all over the land.
So don't pass him by
Without sparing a thought,
The history they have
And by whom it was brought.

Though his triumphs and victories are gone
His foundations they still build upon.
So turn back the hour
And give thanks to his power,
Stan Cullis and his legend live on.

Heroes were in the making for us boys down on the field and football was where they were, also Molineux was drawing us to see the Wolves. Who was my hero? I suppose it was Hughie McIlmoyle, a centre forward from Port Glasgow in Scotland.

I Suppose It Was Hughie McIlmoyle ©

2007

Who started it all?
Your devotion and your pleasure and pain.
Who made you want to go?
And stand in the cold and the winters rain.

When the next fixture came around,
No matter what happened last Saturday.
You make your way to your holy ground,
Today is the day that we call match day.

Why do we all feel the same?
After all, it's only a game.
Why do we all do what we do?
Hands up those who have got a tattoo.

Your feelings don't have a holiday,
They never laze in the sun.
They are not too far out of reach,
This torment sometime must have begun.

I often think back to who started all this,
Before I had learned the pleasure of a kiss.
Someone, somewhere gave this boy,
A lifetime of sadness, excitement and joy.
I sipped and loathed my dad's mild beer
Then all of a sudden it was sorrow and cheer,

If I had to name one who made me loyal,
I suppose it was Hughie McIlmoyle.
So I'll give him the blame,
For attracting me to this great blessed game.
I won't add up to what it's cost,
Whatever life I should have had has been lost.
In my gut is a knot,
That's winding like a coil,
It was definitely Hughie McIlmoyle.

We were happy and growing and toning our skills before the days of organised coaching sessions and lighted areas. It was noticeable that the games were becoming more and more competitive and on occasions we would play against boys from other areas. We found a name and called ourselves Rough Hills Rangers and for whatever reason we chose to play in the blue and white hoops of QPR. Then came a day when we were all stunned.

My Adidas Santiago ©

2007

I recall how bright the floodlights were,
When I played on Fellows Park.
They were nothing quite like the old streetlights,
Where I learned my skills in the dusk and the dark.

My Adidas Santiago gleamed,
And distracted a driver or two.
After tea every day where could I play?
What else could a football youngster do?

The ball that I used sometimes went on the road
And I had to then make chase,
That's where I learned to use my speed
It was where I needed my pace.

I often pass by that same old field
And see boys playing there like I used to do,
I remember the time I heard the news
A Police car had hit and killed Michael Pugh.

He was only chasing a ball,
Now there are bushes and shrubs five feet tall.
Too late to save a young boy who's gone,
Planted where my Adidas Santiago shone.

RIP Michael

In the spring of 2007 work started on erecting a perimeter fence around the Dixon Street playing fields.

Now, allow me to travel forward for just a short while to when approaching my 60th year. The bushes and shrubs around the field have matured and obviously not allowing a ball kicked out of play reach the road unless smacked at a good height.

Coincidently I received a friend request on Facebook and after our messaging conversation about Rough Hills I found that it was Michael Pugh's sister who was aged 5 at the time of the accident. Within days I had received friend requests from other sisters and also his brother Keith. I explained to them that it was the saddest time of my childhood.

A Blessing of a Sunny Sunday Afternoon ©

2013

When all is quiet
like a Sunday afternoon
In the Autumn
on a Sunday afternoon

When we're expecting
wet or cold weather coming soon
we discover
a sunny afternoon

A blessing of
a sunny Sunday afternoon
savour this October
sunny Sunday afternoon

when the field was ours
our voices faded soon,
now the field is theirs
on this sunny Sunday afternoon

I could not believe how nice it was on the first Sunday of October 2013. Warm as a day in June as the sun heated the back of my jacket. I was on the Dixon Street playing fields where 50 years earlier I was there in childhood. A sunny early afternoon game of football sprinkled with spectators in a lovely autumn atmosphere. An elderly gentleman walking the perimeter of the field, children playing on the park and leisurely dog walkers.

It was lovely except the Monkey House was sadly boarded up. It would have been great to have a nostalgic drink and quench my thirst, toasting my shared childhood with all those 'thirty's when the field was ours.

"when the field was ours
our voices faded too soon,
now the field is theirs
on this sunny Sunday afternoon"

I must add that the following Sunday of October the
weather was awful so it truly was a blessing.

The bus from Wolverhampton to the Rough Hills
Estate was the number 30. The stops for us were at the
top or bottom of Cheviot Road and it turned around in
Hardy Square. The journey to town was along Major
Street and Steelhouse Lane passing by All Saints Infant
and Junior School which was opposite St Joseph's. We
had many a snowball war with Joey's in the
wintertime. The bus drove along Bilston Street with the
agriculture machinery sales on the one side of the road
and the bus garage on the other then the Abattoir. It
then went along Pipers Row where we disembarked in
Queens Street, before that the stop was opposite the
Grand Theatre outside of the Co-op store where Santa
Claus was here every Christmas. The ABC cinema was
the place to be for kids on a Saturday morning and the
Arcade with the W. Sherwood Miller toy store. Many a
child has gazed in awe in front of that shop window,
me included.

Most families done their main shopping in the town
and I can recall feeling sorry for my mother when
seeing her walking up the street with two large

shopping bags. She wasn't alone as there were also other women walking as the number 30 bus carried on down the road. For smaller shopping we had Darby's on Dixon Street and Rooker Avenue.

Dixon St, 2014
formerly Darby's

As a lad I liked to run and found an errand a challenge. If it was a chip shop tea we were having my mom would give me the order and off I went. About 200 yards down our road was the garages and an alley that led to a piece of wasteland alongside the Rough Hills Tavern, now sadly adrift and derelict and most probably will soon be gone. That wasteland we called the patch and is now houses. Writing this makes me recall it was a haven for caterpillars and crickets. In Rooker Avenue, which stretched from Dixon Street to Parkfield Road, was a line of shops with the chippy at the far end. I can even remember the first time that they started selling hot sausage rolls. A piece of heaven at the time was sausage roll and chips.

In that line of shops was a grocer, butcher, hairdresser, greengrocer, sweetshop, handy stores and a cobbler. All soon to be affected by the shopping stores to be introduced to towns and villages alike. Also there was the nearest red telephone box to our house now also almost a thing of the past with home and mobile phones.

In later years I was to be informed by a mild natured

gentleman by the name of Roy Fellows, a colleague,
that he used to cut my dad's hair and mine when I was
a boy.

The obvious challenge in the chip shop was how
quickly could I get back home with the family tea.
Years later when in my thirties and in marathon
training I used to run the two and a half miles to work
along Dixon Street every morning passing Rooker
Avenue. I would race against my time and within a
couple of months reduced it dramatically, which had
great affect when next entering a race.

When first built two of those shops were occupied by
my mothers uncle who before that his shop was a hut
on the playing field.

Rooker Avenue Shops, 2013

"Aside the Rough Hills Tavern,
and over the land we called the patch,
the chip shop there I'd reckon,
I could run home in hundred seconds"

Home in Hundred Seconds ©

2009

An errand ran this Cheviot child he jogged there up
the alley,
Aside the Rough Hills Tavern,
And over the land we called the patch.
The chip shop there I'd reckon,
I could run home in hundred seconds.

Rooker 'chippy' had a counter of stainless steel,
Falsified faces reflected then came our meal.
Salt and vinegar showered upon,
Newspaper wrapping then ready and gone.

Dispatch and over the patch back down the alley,
Aiming to beat my tally.
The chip shop there I'd reckon,
I could run home in hundred seconds.

Morality conveyed from boy to man,
Get the job done as best as I can.
Targeting the touch of our outhouse door,
Ninety-two, ninety-three, ninety-four.

An errand ran this Cheviot child he jogged there up
the alley,
Aside the Rough Hills Tavern,
And over the land we called the patch.
The chip shop there I'd reckon,
I could run home in ninety seconds.

Dark evenings in those days seemed to last forever and it was sad to see the playing field pitch black. Occasionally we would attempt to play a game in the dark but as you can imagine we experienced a problem or two. This was before the day of home entertainment and parents need not worry about youngsters playing outside.

We needed to blow off schoolboy steam and there was always excitement in the air when word got about of the Grand National. This is not the famous one at Aintree but it was our race and I have a guilty feeling as writing it because if we were caught we were in trouble.

OUR GRAND NATIONAL ©

2010

Our Grand National
no not the one you think it be,
not the one from Aintree
not the one in Liverpool,
shadows in the night
of the lampost light
we raced and chased after school.

o'er privet and hedges oh yes!
cheeky little beggars I guess,
that race was so inviting
extremely so exciting.

Our Grand National
oh what a race,
cover your tracks
and cover your face

running over gardens
running out of luck,
at the imaginary Chair
and Beeches Brook

jockey's without a horse
nor stirrups and saddles but
we had a course

our Grand National
not the one but it was to us
juvenile delinquent's
to some on the number 30 bus

Our Grand National
no not the one you think it be,
not the one from Aintree,
around about eight o'clock
kids went running around the block.

Wolverhampton Marathon on Dixon Street in 1986
with the MEB offices in the background

"The MEB has gone
I think of who I am
and where I'm from"

The MEB Has Gone poem was completed on the first day of school of my second eldest Grandson. I wonder what memories he shall have?

My story poem of how areas of upbringing change in one way or another and what a person learns and passes on. Good and bad influences in a youngsters life can make a dramatic difference.

Upon researching and speaking to my mother about Steelhouse Lane she reminded me of where she was born and of a story that was passed down to her of the cinder wall. Accordingly my nan was pleased to see that it had not been demolished with the redevelopment of the area as she could remember it in her younger days.

Who shall carry the can for who I am? The answer could be parents, family, friends who walked together in early years of life. Educating each other and learning right from wrong. Perhaps God himself had something to do with it?

The MEB Has Gone ©

2012

The Monkey House is boarded up and empty
changes are a plenty

The MEB has gone
I think of who I am and where I'm from

and who shall carry the can for who I am?

run once more on Dixon Street once more,
down Dixon Street up Major Street once more

down Dixon Street up Major Street
with youngsters feet once more

seems yesterday my first school day
up Major Street
past the twin peaked wall at Bayliss's
Bayliss Jones Bayliss's

the 'Monkey' alias the Moulders Arms
the fence around the football ground
the double gates
at Bayliss's
Bayliss Jones Bayliss's

The MEB has gone
I think of who I am and where I'm from

and who shall carry the can for who I am?

Caledonia Store was opposite Adey's
customers came on Steelhouse Lane from Bayliss's
Bayliss Jones Bayliss's

was it Marandola's doors that I recall?
the cinder wall seemed trait and tall
near the Summerhouse on Steelhouse Lane,
All Saints
where a register had my name.

how strange, a register had my name?

The MEB has gone
I think of who I am and where I'm from

and who shall carry the can for who I am?

run once more on Dixon Street once more,
down Dixon Street up Major Street once more

Cable Street and Eagle Street
with youngsters feet once more

and who shall carry the can for who I am?

confided and then guided me from boy to man,
and walked with me on streets
where I once ran?

and who shall carry the can for who I am,
and help scatter the contents
of that battered old can?

It was whilst standing alone in the bar at the Bull in Codsall watching the television and seeing a piper play the bagpipes at the Commonwealth Games 2014 in Glasgow. My Scotland roots surfaced and all of a sudden I was in my childhood home in Cheviot Road.

Hogmanay was always special in our house and neighbours in the street, especially those that I have mentioned when we first arrived, made a great welcome to the new year. Andy Stewart will always be legendary in my world because of Hogmanay and also his song, A Scottish Soldier, as this was always in the air at our home. The opening chords still 'hang on in there' many years later. Brian Ruscoe and I, from two doors down, soon got in to the Hogmanay spirit if I recall correct!

ANDY STEWART SANG ON HOGMANAY ©

2007

Our childhood house was merry on the night of New
Years Eve.
Andy Stewart sang on Hogmanay,
Kilted ladies danced the year away.
All were joyous on the night of New Years Eve.

Our childhood house was merry on the night of New
Years Eve.
My parents were radiant with joy,
Yes they were in the eyes of this wee boy.
There were friendly neighbour wishes,
Shaking of hands and kisses,
All were joyous on the night of New Years Eve.

Our childhood house was merry on the night of New
Years Eve.
Andy Stewart sang on Hogmanay,
Kilted ladies danced the year away.
All were joyous on the night of New Years Eve.

Boscobel House

"A welcome meal of bread and cheese,
in Boscobel House,
a charitable bed.
Charles in hiding changed his plans,
in disguise to France he fled"

Unless time as misted my memory I think that my first school trips were around 1963-64. One was to Moseley Old Hall and the other was to Boscobel House. I still have a postcard from that era.

"An old postcard reminded me of a school trip way
back in 1963,
a cuppa on the table is increasingly getting cold,
my need of glasses shows I'm growing old.."
"Tabletops and memories,
days of trips galore,
I reach for my glasses to study the postcard more"

In October 2013 I found that a Grandson of mine was also going to Boscobel on his school trip so I printed the poem below for him to take to school. "Been there, seen it and got the ….postcard!

Boscobel ©

2007

Defeated at the battle of Worcester,
To London he planned to flee.
Run like the wind young vigorous Charles,
Oliver Cromwell is after thee.

The year of 1651,
Charles lost his fight, where had he gone?

Charles sought shelter at Boscobel House,
Hiding in branches of a huge Oak tree.
They're looking for you young vigorous Charles,
Oliver Cromwell is after thee.

A welcome meal of bread and cheese,
In Boscobel House, a charitable bed.
Charles in hiding changed his plans,
In disguise to France he fled.

The year was 1658,
When Charles heard news of Cromwell's fate.

Two years passed after Cromwell died,
Charles II need not now hide.
Out of exile he then came,
His exploits famed Boscobel name.
In the 1660s the King was he,
Thanks to the shelter of the Royal Oak Tree.

Afterwards I was to hear that my Grandson had
wanted to take a piece of bark for his Grandad from
the tree but was not allowed.

East Park Paddling Pool 2014 during restoration

"six weeks off school
and the East Park paddling pool,
there was many of us
why? Cause the summers were hot
and bet me not
there, was the place to be
for a 1960's kid like me"

Six weeks off school and it's time to head for the East Park 1960's style. Without doubt this was the next best thing to going to the seaside. Excitement would be in the air as word got around that we were to get a towel and trunks as we were off to the East Park.

It's strange how life can sometimes spring surprises. I had penned this poem about a childhood memory of going to the East Park paddling pool to hear the very same paddling pool mentioned 3 days later in a reading for a celebration of Yasmin Bates's life in All Saints Church, Sedgley.

Yasmin from Fieldhouse Road who attended Springvale Juniors and Parkfields also loved going there.

The East Park Paddling Pool ©

2012

And a load of us
trekked down the road
at Dixon Street,
happy little faces, happy little feet

six weeks off school
and the East Park paddling pool

there was many of us
why? Cause the summers were hot
and bet me not
there, was the place to be
for a 1960's kid like me

laugh oh aye as we passed Matt's Cafe
Speedway bikes there out at the back
maintenance, spanners and pliers
autographs, Dugmores bicycle tyre's

that gang of us
giving up keeping calm
with a towel and trunks
rolled under our arm

six weeks off school
and the East Park paddling pool

Park gates are now in sight
this was our Buckingham Palace alright!
down past Monmore Greyhound track
always longer on the road going back

running on fast past the bandstand
gunning for the top of the steps
here was the place to be
for a 1960's kid like me

swings, slides and sunbathers
all shapes and sizes
Punch and Judy
ice cream, Lucky Bag surprises

our towels claimed a piece of ground
all kind o' kids were around
ruffians, scruffy uns, counting
stripped off and heading for the fountain

six weeks off school
and the East Park paddling pool

never missed a chance
never missed a trick
on the witches hat
'till we felt quite sick

six weeks off school
and the East Park paddling pool

and a load of us
trekked up the road
to Dixon Street,
clean little faces, clean little feet

there till the dusk or dark
in a Wolverhampton suburb
down on the East Park

It was sad reading in the Express & Star in August 2012 that Geo Dugmore's cycles in Bilston Road, Monmore Green had closed after more than 108 years. This shop was a part of my childhood as a bike for Christmas was chosen a couple or so times. I could smell the tyres as I entered the shop. Remarkably the business had been passed down 3 generations serving many a Wulfrunian for over a century. Mom and Dad had a account and paid a weekly amount towards the bikes that they brought.

In July of 2007 I returned to the towpaths near where I had grown up to see if my memory had served me correct. This was the first day of the school holidays and most parts of the country was suffering torrential rain. My first stop with brolly in hand was on the Bilston Road of Wolverhampton where I was greeted by a suspicious swan who followed my every move.

Keeping a careful eye on the swan I searched with no luck for rope grooves in the bricks but found some in the steel corner sanctions.

I decided to keep faith in my search and not to be

defeated by driving to the next canal bridge at Horsley Fields. There, as plain as they were many years ago were the grooves in the old corner brick. Again as I had done all those years ago, I imagined the horses pulling the barges laden with heavy loads.

The canal in those days were an important part of the countries industry with many companies setting up alongside. Answering my question in my poem, I do now know that the grooves are still there today, and obviously, man relied on the old trusty horse.

"We studied the grooves
in the old corner brick,
they were cut from the ropes
an inch or more thick,
when horses pulled barges
along the path side"

Grooves

in the Old Corner Brick ©

2004

There was no river for us to walk alongside
But a towpath by the cut
Our bikes we could ride.
And we cycled for hours and hours
We would shelter
Under bridges in showers.
We studied the grooves in the old corner brick,
They were cut from the ropes
An inch or more thick.
When horses pulled barges
Along the path side,
Was they bred to do this
Until the day that they died?
Was it cruel or did they have strength?
How heavy are barges
And what is their length?

155

We'd watch the bargemen
Operate the loch,
And on occasions they'd wave
And pull over to dock.
The towpath was a lesson in time,
When cargo was delivered
By a barge on a line.
And the grooves that we saw in the old corner brick,
That was cut from the ropes
An inch or more thick.
I don't know if they're still there today
It's been many a year
Since I've been there to play.
And that age in time
I imagined of course,
Man relied on the old trusty horse.

Dixon Street 2014

"flow you rolling river,
OK you are a canal,
but listen pal,
the canal was my rolling river"

Listen Pal, the Canal Was my Rolling River ©

Flow you rolling river,
OK you are a canal,
but listen pal,
the canal was my rolling river

The Coseley way or Dunstall
my rolling river was my canal
yes listen pal,
the canal was my rolling river

Every son and daughter
the nearest stretch of water,
one mile was within,
for every clan and kin

Every Rough Hills family
with youngsters just like me,
with bricks we'd skim the cut
if brave we'd dangle a foot

Flow you rolling river,
OK you are a canal,
but listen pal,
the canal was my rolling river

Ships were really barges
there's no sentences or charges,
for me imagining so
to the sea those ships would go

Where else was a rolling river?
sails needing mastering on a yacht,
there is no rolling river
the canal is all I got

Flow you rolling river,
OK you are a canal,
but listen pal,
the canal was my rolling river

Our nearest river was the Severn at Bridgnorth about 14 miles or so away from our house. We were lucky as we had a relation who had a caravan there and our cousins knew the hideouts. Old family photos show us playing down by the embankment among trees. It surely opened up many a youngsters imaginative mind.

The Author at Bridgnorth 1957

Bridgnorth On The Severn ©

2007

Time spent where the Severn flows,
a quaint old market town.
Bridgnorth on the Severn,
a piece of childhood heaven.

Deep down is stored a memory,
the river where I longed to be.
Bridgnorth on the Severn,
a piece of childhood heaven.

On banks and branches of temptress trees,
I climbed, explored and scraped my knees.
Watching rising of ripple as the river did flow,
throw a twig in the water and wonder,
yes I wondered how far it would go?

When descending down Hermitage hill,
the sight of High Town excites me still.
Bridgnorth on the Severn,
a piece of childhood heaven.

Dixon Street, 2014

"over the top of the Embankment,

on the way to the Speedway,

I couldn't prevent,

myself running up the embankment"

The Dixon Street Embankment ©

2014

Three or four steps up this embankment,
on the way to Eastfield,
over the top of the embankment,
on the way to Eastfield,
also to the Speedway,
the roar and smell of the Speedway,
over the top of the Embankment,
on the way to the Speedway,
I couldn't prevent,
myself running up the embankment,
on the way to the East Park,
Eastfields or the Speedway,
Robbie had a field day,
on the way to the Speedway

How can a young laddie who was later to run marathons, walk the Fife Coastal Path, not be tempted to go the hardest way round to get to where he was going.

I have wrote of roots and places in Scotland and Wolverhampton, St Peters Church to the Forth Rail Bridge and more. Soon I shall be travelling my 5 hour journey to connect to my Scottish ancestral side but now, my growing-up years, All Saints, Rough Hills and Wolverhampton.

I write this when listening to lovely songs about Belfast, Dublin and Galway. There, is the reason why I write of my upbringing. I do not feel that I have missed out in life, I am a pupil of All Saints and Eastfield, not a clever one I may add.

Many, many times I have drove past a small grassed area of Dixon Street and recalled this as a challenge. I have to question as to why I am writing about a small incline and piece of grass?

Well, that's me, a Rough Hills lad, running up a Dixon

Street embankment, proud as to be writing about as
the Forth Rail Bridge.

We became amateur astrologers as I wrote of earlier,
as many dark nights were spent outside in the street
gazing at the sky. Names and formations have long
been forgotten but not the Plough. To this day
whenever I see a starlit sky the Plough is what I look
for and when found within a second my mind is back
on the streets of the Rough Hills.

"Sorting out the stars
and searching for the Plough,
I become that kid again
when I'm looking for it now"

Millers Bridge on Dixon Street seemed to be an endless job when they demolished the narrow one to be replaced by the canal bridge that is today. I would be at secondary school and had to carry my bike up and over the footbridge or cycle the long way round to Cable Street. Just below the Millers Bridge is the railway bridge where once or maybe more a bus attempted to drive under. This caused major disruption to commuters as inspectors had to give the bridge the all clear.

Nearing Christmas a mate and myself would earn a bit of money by going from house to house singing carols. We didn't have the nerve to sing in our street so very often it would be Cotswold or Durberville Road. There were many households that chose not to answer the door and some paid for us to move on. I recollect that this carol singer partner later became a bouncer around the bars in town and whenever I hear his name it brings a smile.

Rough Hill Rail Bridge, 2014

"Barges and folk they came
and we waved,
not knowing their name,
like a meeting with an old friend
then out of sight
around the canal bend"

Down on Durberville Road ©

2014

Shouldn't have done but we did,
in this ode I lift the lid,
we ventured too close to the railway,
down on Durberville Road

That was those days
we had no fear,
that was that time
our yesteryear

We got through by the council garages,
myself and many a pal,
explorers we were under the railway bridge
alongside the Birmingham Canal

Barges and folk they came
and we waved, not knowing their name,
like a meeting with an old friend
then out of sight around the canal bend

We skimmed the stones across the cut,
dip a toe or dangle a foot,
occasionally someone fell in
the brave would jump in and swim

That was those days
we had no fear,
that was that time
our yesteryear

Trains rumbled and blared,
pennies got stretched if you dared,
in this ode I lift the lid,
shouldn't have done but we did,
down on Durberville Road

I returned in 2014 to take a photograph but a gate
prevented the access to the garages that were once
there in my young days. Later I parked-up on the
Ettingshall Road to walk up the drive to the canal. Half
way up I noticed a Barge passing by so I ran the short
distance to catch it in a picture. Having not been there
for over 48 years or so I thought that the canal was not
as wide as I remembered. Within seconds came the
rumble of an approaching train. Then came 48 year
old feelings as the train went over the bridge. I felt as
though I had stepped back into my childhood.

"Trains rumbled and blared,
pennies got stretched if you dared,
in this ode I lift the lid,
shouldn't have done but we did,
down on Durberville Road"

Parkfield Road, 2014

"Off we went
towards Durberville Road,
around by Hardy Square,
we came to the junction at Vale Street
over the road we could see it there"

When The Fair Came to Parkfield Road ©

2014

Children went crazy
lively one's and the lazy,
word soon spread on the street,
get some money in your pocket
and shoes on your feet

My mates dad worked at John Thompson
give a man his due,
posters were on the billboards
that's my recollection of how we knew

Off we went towards Durberville Road,
around by Hardy Square,

we came to the junction at Vale Street
over the road we could see it there

The Fair was there on Parkfield Road
on Parkfield Road the Fair was there

it was there, it was really there

Kid's were coming out of Myrtle Street too
the Fair was there, oh what a view!

From every house with every name,
the children came,
from every school and every class,
the children came

All Saints, Rough Hills and Parkfields
Ettingshall, Coseley and Lanesfield,
the children came

Bilston and Millfields
the children came

When the Fair came to Parkfield Road,
to Parkfield Road the Fair came

….so did the children

Kid's went home
with excitement in their eye's,
all spent out
some carried a prize

when the Fair came

When the Fair went from Parkfield Road
from Parkield Road the Fair went,

Leaving flattened ground
a new destination bound,
the Fair was gone
and normal life carried on

Rooker Avenue from Dixon Street to Parkfield Road seemed a long way when a lad but may in truth be only half-a-mile if that. Beyond where the Rough Hills Tavern was on the left (demolished in 2014) and playing fields to the right was a strange sight. The tarmac road ended and a dirt road began and was about 200 yards or so to the junction at Parkfield Road.

At the start of the dirt road to the right aside the playing fields was Parkfield Iron and Steel. Accordingly my mother told me that her brother declined the opportunity to go into business with this company. The offices were a large wooden hut and I can recall that my mother was a cleaner there.

I seem to remember that the road being as such was because it was a boundary between Wolverhampton and Bilston Council although I stand to be corrected if not so. The dirt road with the ruts was brilliant for us lad's to ride in and out of on our bikes especially after a good shower. We imagined ourselves to be motorcycle scramblers that were popular at the time and on TV most Saturday afternoons.

Ruts in the Dirt Road on Rooker Avenue ©

2014

Little footprints
were seen in the ruts,
in the ruts on the dirt road,
down on Rooker Avenue

The ruts
in the dirt road,
became puddles,
that grew and grew

Lad's did like
riding through
ruts and puddles
on their bike

Near Parkfield Road
where memories stack,
cars, lorries and motorbikes
to Bilston and back

Tyre tracks too
as the puddles grew and grew
because of teeming rain
we were adventurers once again

Ruts and puddles,
little footprints
once upon a time,
children of the area
they were yours and mine,
ruts and puddles,
little footprints
from a bygone time

OUR CASTLES WERE TALL
AS THE SEA FRONT WALL ©

2004

Do you remember what I can remember?
The sun and the sea and the sand,
Can you recall what I can recall?
The stands with the big brass band.
The walks we had with our mom and our dad
And our kites were as high as the sun,
In the wind it did blow the beach ball did flow
The chase we had to then run.
Our castles were tall as the sea front wall
But we left them behind for tomorrow,

179

And then we did find what we left behind
Had gone and we felt a bit sorrow.
But we'd start off again in the wind and the rain
We'd build out of sand our new towers,
And gone was the rain when teatime came
The sun had been shining for hours.
Our shoulders felt sore so a tee shirt we wore
So we could all be safe and be healthy,
What I'm trying to reach is life on the beach
Is for the rich the poor and the wealthy.
So when we are old and our stories are told
We may find it hard to remember,
But I still recall and can you still recall?
We went back to school in September.

Times were changing as it was soon to be out there in the real world to work for a living. I had tasted a wee bit of maturity by having had a couple of jobs as a paperboy. The first shop I worked for was Cartwrights in Monmore Green and I had not so much of a pleasure of being bitten by a nasty German Shepherd in Stowheath. In later years I was to be the owner of three of that breed and social inclusion and good ownership is paramount.

Soon afterwards I was to move for better wages to another shop at the top end of Parkfield Road near to Gills and Thompson Avenue. The round that became mine was along the Birmingham New Road around the estate by Parkfield School. Within a few years I entered into another stage of my life in the same area having met a girl at a youth club.

Before then I had started work, still playing football, gained trials at various football clubs, signed for Walsall FC and walked away about 6 months later. I am often asked if I regret that decision but it put me on a path to the family that I have today so the answer has to be no.

Delta, Bilston Road, 2014

When Lynne and I were courting
she would sometimes meet me after work at the gate

I was to meet all types of characters in my early working life and one of them was first to be put into print many years later. I was in my teens and working at Delta Rods in Monmore Green, Wolverhampton. Within this place of work there were many characters of which some have helped me to mould myself to the man that I am today.

One of those characters was Fred Lowbridge, a Surface Grinder working in the tool room. I was told that he was a boxer when he was a young man. It was now early 1970's and he would be in his sixties. A good 15 years or so had passed and I was working at Yale Material Handling in Wednesfield when I decided to write a poem about Fred.

My family and I moved house to Codsall, just outside of Wolverhampton in 1986 and settled into the local community. One day in a local pub a gentleman named as Fred Lowbridge was pointed out to me. 'That's not Fred Lowbridge, I informed, he's not old enough'. It so happened that it was Fred's son, also named Fred. I got to know him over the years as I did many other locals who all knew me as Bob.

I was unfortunately made redundant in the 1980's and made a career change into insurance. One of my customers was named Ray Lowbridge and I mentioned to him that I had written a poem about Fred Lowbridge who happened to be his dad. I am not sure if it was my imagination as it didn't seem to make much of an impression upon him. Perhaps he was thinking I was a 'crack pot' as they said in the old days.

In July of 1996, almost 5 years since I had wrote it, I heard that a local nostalgic newspaper called the Black Country Bugle had printed it. Well young Fred then telephoned Ray to tell him that a poem about their dad written by someone called Robbie Bennett was in the Bugle. Ray then told him that I knew him and lived in Codsall. Fred then realised it was me; 'oh it's Bob the footballer' he said. On the Thursday afternoon young Fred came to visit me at home. 'You've made a family proud' he told me, 'my mother has said it is him to a tee'. I was shocked to find that she was still alive and into her 90's.

Young Fred has now passed on and I introduced myself to his widow at Alf Perry's funeral. She was pleasantly surprised to meet me and complimented me on the poem. She also told me how proud Fred was when he saw it in print.

FRED LOWBRIDGE ©

1991

I studied old Fred has he worked
A fellow so gentle and kind,
Private and so inoffensive
No finer a man can you find.
Fred Lowbridge they said was a fighter
In days of being a young man
I ask myself can I imagine
I have to admit that I can.
In the bugle I often read stories
Of fights in days of old,
Fred fought in a league of true sportsman
Boxers so brave and so bold.
Prize money was coppers and shillings
Recovery time was short,
No sooner the bout was over
Another opponent was sought.
Fred's hands looked like they'd fought many
His face must have sometimes been hurt,
Fred Lowbridge a man I admired
He quietly got on with his work.

It was more or less from here that I realised that writing can have a good affect on many a persons life and over 20 years later new odes of mine still appear.

Back to the late 1960's, didn't learn much for the first few years of my working life as social activities were regular as the disco scene had taken a grip on the nation. In that scene was the girlfriend of mine and settling down was next in line. We were to have a lengthy teenage courtship and married at an age that frightens me more today than it did then. Too young springs to mind but almost 40 years later we still share our lives with a marriage, children and grandchildren.

Early in the season of 1969-70 the footballing world was to receive the news that Peter Knowles, Wolves talented England U23 player was to retire for religious reasons. He played his last game at Molineux on 3rd September 1969. To this day Peter is still held in high regard as he was idolised by the thousands and a great loss to the football club.

Yorkshire born, Knowles signed aged 17 from Wath Wanderers and was a gifted player that appeared to have a bright future. There were great doubts that he would finish his career at such a young age but he was true to his word. His registration was held for another 12 years until the club conceded that he would not return.

Although hurtful to all Supporters of the football club it was also painful for me in another way. The game itself was against Nottingham Forest and ended up 3-3 after Wolves were leading 3-0 at half-time. I was on my way home after the game and wearing a coloured jumper that could have been looked upon as Wolves. By the side the Art Gallery in St Peters Walk a group of opposing supporters were suddenly upon me from the church gardens. I was alone and well and truly out numbered and one hit in my face injected my schoolboy cross country champion instinct. I sprinted as fast as I could along the walk and straight across Lichfield Street to the alley opposite with almost another direct hit from a bus. It was only when I got as far as Pipers Row that I eased off the pace. Peter may have said goodbye but I was not hanging around to say so long to that lot.

When Peter Said Goodbye ©

2007

When Peter said goodbye,
Tears appeared in a golden eye.
Talent emerges once in a while,
No one dared to smile.

When Peter said farewell,
Was it forever, no one could tell.
They sung with praise his name,
And had their doubts he would leave the game.

When Peter said so long,
If they disbelieved, then they were wrong.
Peter will come back very soon,
They kept his place in the dressing room.

Peter never returned,
He gave them notice, a lesson learned.
When Peter said goodbye,
The young and the old couldn't understand why.
When Peter walked away,
Gold dust was lost that day.

I was about 15 years of age and going to Hilton Road to play football for the Youth Club on the pitches directly behind the hall. From then I started attending the youth club here and at nearby Parkfields School. It eventually led to me meeting my wife to be.

Once again I wanted to write a new ode so I decided to get thinking about that time in my life. I mention in my poem of taking a photo of Hilton Hall as it is at the time of writing and I planned to do so as soon as possible. I parked up over the road hoping that there were no vehicles outside of the hall to spoil the picture. I couldn't help but be impressed with how smart it looked. I stood by the roadside imagining me as a youth going up and down the ramp and in at out of the door.

I moved to take a picture of the football pitches to find that there is now a BMX track at the near end of the field. Obviously there has been plenty of hard work done in and around the hall. Within a few seconds a fellow in a Scotland cap came from the building and introduced himself to me as Keith Jones.

He spoke of how volunteers worked to save the hall and invited me inside to see the result of their work. Not only was my mind active with recalling my youthful days in the hall, I was highly impressed with their story which is on their website in more detail. Because of their efforts the Hilton Hall and surroundings will reach another generation or so of youngsters.

I could tell that Keith was busy doing his work but still he took the time to show me around the hall.

It was late last night that I had thought of writing of Hilton Hall and within 12 hours I had found a success story worthy of being written about.

Hilton Hall, 2014

"near the Birmingham New Road
in Lanesfield,
there's a hall with a sloping roof
Hilton Road Youth Club
I'll go take a picture
as I need some proof"

HILTON ROAD YOUTH CLUB at HILTON HALL ©

2014

Disco lights they flashed
pretty teenage girls
ran on and off of the dance floor

near the Birmingham New Road in Lanesfield,
there's a hall with a sloping roof
Hilton Road Youth Club
I'll go take a picture as I need some proof

on the dance floor
us boys we stood on the outside,
daring each other to be brave to
venture on to the inside,

195

to dance with the teenage girls,
that I told you of before,
those pretty girls
they're now dancing on the dance floor

and to me the prettiest teenage girl,
running on and off of the dance floor,
she was the prettiest girl in the Youth Club
she'll be the prettiest for evermore,
at Hilton Road, and any old dance floor

It was now in the early 1970's and many a weekend was spent dancing at the Ship and Rainbow on the Dudley Road. The Tamla Motown sound had taken a hold of a big percentage of youngsters of our age. Settling down was to be the obvious plan but at times love can be misunderstanding.

TURN BACK TIME ©

1993

Someone said in the crowd today
Never ever let her see you that way.
Wipe those tears
Dry your eyes,
It's good advice 'cause he does sound wise.

It seems like only yesterday
Turn back time you will hear me say.
Does she hurt?
Is she sad?
If she is then should I be glad.

We only had a quarrel
We only had a fight,
It turned all over in my head last night.

I wonder if she fell asleep in bed
Or did those words turn inside her head.
Does her heart
Hurt like mine?
If I could only turn back time.

Someone said in the crowd today
Never ever let her see you that way.
Show your tough
That you're strong,
You'll soon forget her it won't take long.

But if her heart
Hurts like mine,
Then I wish I could turn back time.

After work and teatime I set off most evenings to meet my girlfriend who lived about a twenty five minute walk away near to Parkfields School. Sometimes I would walk to the Parkfield Road and over waste ground that brought me out on Hilton Road. Most often it would be up Dixon Street and along Thompson Avenue and the Birmingham New Road occasionally calling into relations as I was passing.

An early childhood memory of visiting this Aunt and Uncle's house to see them and my cousins is in a poem of mine. Uncle Ern would sometimes take me a walk down his garden to show me the plants he was growing.

The daily activity of people and vehicles on the main road was fascinating for a 'wee laddie' like me. The bus from Wolverhampton would stop for a while by the flowerbed before turning around and heading back to town. The Midland Red also passed by but carried on along the Birmingham New Road.

On these visits I often asked my Aunt Mill if she had an 'opple' to eat. I loved the taste of a sour cooking 'opple!

When older, I would occasionally bump into my Uncle Ern and have a pint with him in either the Red Lion or the Parkfield Tavern. Both pub's now are other business's denying me a nostalgic drink whenever I am this side of Wolverhampton.

Now, when driving by the house, I always have a sea of memories flooding back. God bless Shaz.

Thompson Avenue, 2008

"She lived on a busy main road
at Thompson Avenue
opposite a flowerbed
where pretty flowers grew"

The Pretty Flower Bed at
Thompson Avenue ©

2008

Just a wee lad with a watchful eye
Visiting my Aunt Mill's house
Where cars and lorries drove on by

She lived on a busy main road
At Thompson Avenue
Opposite a flowerbed
Where pretty flowers grew

A bus would stop a few minutes or so
And to Wolverhampton town would go
It circled around the flowerbed
At Thompson Avenue
The pretty, pretty flower bed
Where pretty flowers grew.

It circled around the flowerbed
At Thompson Avenue
The pretty, pretty flower bed
Where pretty flowers grew.

The pretty, pretty flower bed
Where pretty flowers grew.
Where my pretty, pretty cousins lived
On Thompson Avenue.

For a few years up to his retirement I worked with a humorous good-natured man called Len Muir. Without doubt this man taught me a lot about life and not to take it too seriously. He was in his sixties and I would be about twenty and we formed a great partnership. We worked together in a two-man department cleaning extrusion dies for a 2000 ton press at Delta Rods in Monmore Green, Wolverhampton.

I had been selected to work with Len for the last two years or so up to his retirement. When the day came it was a happy sad one as we both knew that it was over. I can recall being in the canteen for his presentation. He tried to make light of his last day and working life was never to be the same again.

Old Len Muir Was Funny ©

2004

Old Len Muir was funny
So much my sides would ache,
He humoured me
With my mug of tea
Before I was even awake.

He would tell me funny stories
Of his days in younger years,
A comical bloke
With time for a joke,
Even though retirement nears.

I can see him riding through Monmore Green
Before eight then half past four,
He gave me happy memories
That I will keep forever more.

Len Muir was the funniest of friends
Where ever I have toiled,
We would start our day
And laugh away
While the kettle boiled.

He would dress in a change of clothes
And his false teeth he would shed,
He'd fool those he'd known for many years.
With a wig upon his head.

When I was twenty-one
And Len was sixty-four,
We worked along
And sang our song,
That I will sing forever more.

The years passed by and time went on
After Len retired,
I grew on through fatherhood
But old Len I still admired.

That saddest day that came my way,
With news that he'd passed on,
His smile his outlook and humour
…My funny friend had gone.

The last time that I saw old Len
Nearing ninety and still so bright,
Soon I paid my last respect
To a sparkling shining light.

We worked upon a factory floor
Our duties we did tend,
Through tears of endless laughter
I made a lifetime's friend.

Len Muir was a man who cared for not only me in my young adult years when working together but afterwards when having children. He took great interest in my life and I will never forget him. Len was extremely interested in me as a person and also my family. He was nearing 90 years old when he finally departed this life. Prior to that I had dropped by to visit him to show him my daughter and son aged about 8 and 6.

Out of our time together came a lesson to help the young on their way at a place of work.

"When I was twenty-one
and Len was sixty-four,
we worked along
and sang our song,
that I will sing forever more"

Factory life and the shop floor can be a world of amusement and education as it links together all types of people. Some cannot take to a place of work and move on at the earliest opportunity and there are those who stay for life. In later years I was to experience the sight of grown men in tears because of redundancy.

The Right to Stand Tall ©

2006

The common decency of the working class
Is a jewel in the crown and should never let pass
It has gave the strength to fight many wars
To keep things clean and do all chores
It has woke at dawn or worked through the night
It should know when to reason and settle a fight
It has no airs but perhaps has graces
It is noticed whenever in grand places
So whatever you feel
as you walk through your next door
You've a right to stand tall as your father before.

There were an abundance of characters in workplaces where I have been fortunate to find employment. Many a joke or rumour spread like wild fire from department to department. The maintenance at one work had an ex-wrestler so he would be showing his strangle holds, another was a dab-hand at card-tricks and we had Frenchie who could balance a bike on his chin! Yes you heard correct, he could balance a bike on his chin!!!

A Personality by The Name of Frenchie Pearson ©

2009

A crowd had gathered on the factory floor
Making me want to find what for
Maintenance men arrived with tools
A place of work links professors, all faiths and fools

Out of that crowd that were standing there
Appeared two wheels ten feet in the air
"Come and have look" called my old mate Len
So I pushed to the front of a dozen men

Frenchie was balancing a bike
By the saddle upon his chin
Frenchie a personality
A worn face with a cheerful grin

He also wove tubular chairs
From bundles of industrial string
Frenchie a personality
Entertained and done many strange things

He fitted and lubricated red hot dies
On the B5 extrusion press
A breakdown occurrence and men were bored
What Frenchie did was anyone's guess.

Now may I add as a matter of fact
Frenchie done a turn like a circus act
Len made off to go fetch his bike
A pair of old comedians
That was what they were like

Frenchie spun the bike on the ground
Then lifted it high-up in the air

Men soon gathered in a crowd all around
They soon all gathered there

Frenchie was balancing a bike
By the saddle upon his chin
Frenchie a personality
A worn face with a comical grin

One more priceless piece
In my meandering memory bank
Factory days of taking the 'Mick'
And open to the juvenile prank,

The crowd dispersed on the factory floor
Completed it had of what they'd stopped for,
Maintenance men walked away with tools
A place of work links professors, all faiths and fools

Reading the ode about my old mate Len Muir takes me back to those days and earlier. I had obviously missed my chance of ever making it to the rank of being a professional footballer when walking away from Walsall. The remainder of my teenage years was spent bedding into factory life until a certain amateur footballer nearing the veteran stage talked me into signing for his team. I did so and by the end of that season of 1973-74 was awarded the Player of the Year at the Black Horse Public House on Thompson Avenue.

I can recall the evening very well as it was our wedding the next day. My Father-in-Law to be collected my fiancée for the last time of me seeing her until meeting to share our vows in a Church within a mile away. We married and settled down and myself being a competitive young man, always wanting to stand my ground sometimes got me into the occasional confrontation. The Scottish blood inside of me didn't help matters!

Our Honeymoon was in Eileen's caravan, (Mom's next door neighbour), Clarach Bay, Near Aberystwyth in Wales. I can recall Gareth my elder brother driving us there in his 3 x wheeler Reliant and Dad picking us up one week later in his Austin Cambridge. It was a strange feeling throughout as although we had made our commitment to each other in marriage, to have only each others company for full days and nights had its challenges. What I do remember is playing games of cards in a rainy caravan and the entertainment in the clubhouse on the evening. The most memorable time of the week was when Lynne was presented with a pair of tights when winning the Miss Lovely Legs competition.

That was in 1974 and around 11 years later we were to return to Clarach Bay with our young children accompanied by Lynne's parents. We have some lovely photographs of that holiday and we most probably stayed at my brothers caravan at Capel Bangor.

Now, I have the experience of looking through the eyes of a father of a girl. My wife to be was still only 17 years of age when we married so understandably there must have been doubts of our commitment towards each other.

'Hag' my Father-in-Law, Bilston born.

"Did her dad disapprove
the day we were wed?
When he sat with our kids
and put them to bed.
And didn't he often come
looking for me,
to find out where I was likely to be"

Her Dad Disapproved ©

2006

When we first met we were young and carefree,

She was a little bit younger than me.

And we went to the youth club dance,

Her dad disapproved of our youthful romance.

Then all of a sudden we were wed,

A few years passed before we wet a babe's head.

Did her dad disapprove of our youthful romance?

He played with our kids when we went out and dance.

Did her dad disapprove the day we were wed?

When he sat with our kids and put them to bed.

And didn't he often come looking for me,

To find out where I was likely to be.

And I brought him a pint when he found where I were,

A dinnertime drink I could never deter.
We played the football pools together,
He worked on my house in all kind of weather.
We went to the seaside and backed a slow horse,
It should've done better
when raced around the course.
Did her dad disapprove the day we were wed?
I heard about me that he had once said.
I was the son that he'd never had,
To come from Hag it couldn't be bad.

Mentioning the Black Horse, two days after taking photographs, our local paper, The Express and Star, reported metal theft etcetera from the Black Horse. According to the report, in May 2006 this was the first pub in the city to have its licence revoked. This once magnificent building has fallen into disrepair with local residents and campaigners awaiting the council's decision regarding its future.

It was eventually demolished with new houses built upon the site. It is still a point of reference when giving people direction as only last night (2013) I said, "do you remember where the Black Horse was? The answer was "yes". It was sad to see the pub go as around 40 years earlier we had many good evenings there when courting and early married life.

In the early days of our marriage we had a couple of British summer holidays with friends of ours. Phil had grown up with me on the Rough Hills and his wife Lynne was also a friend of my wife. So we were close and had plenty in common like going to the Disco's that were on at the Ship and Rainbow on the Dudley Road. They were to marry and had their wedding reception at the Black Horse and I was to be Phil's Best Man. One of those holidays was at Looe in Cornwall and I can remember them putting a chair up against their bedroom door as they found that I was doing a bit of sleep walking. Phil at the time was driving a Triumph Vitesse which was a soft-top and quite low. So low that it scraped the bottom badly when we were boarding the ferry at Fowey. Another holiday started with us setting out overnight and the four of us sleeping in a mini. Phil was to later take over his dad's decorating business and when I was coaching my sons football team in the 1990's he became their sponsor.

Black Horse, Thompson Avenue, 2008
now demolished

"My concerns are now recorded,
are bulldozers moving in?
Classify thereby
a mere shame and not a sin"

The Day of The Pub ©
2008

Redundantly adrift in the community,
Observe my reader and you will see,
Pubs are closed and boarded,
My concerns are now recorded.
Are bulldozers moving in?
Classify thereby a mere shame and not a sin.
The British pub is sadly on its knees,
Is it now last orders please?
To the modern day majority,
Have they lost their popularity?
A decision now a pending?
An institution ending?
At the very least I've had my say
Perhaps the pub has had its day.

To make a house homely is a mothers pride and the force of nature can have a devastating affect. This happened one year when living with my wife's parents. There had been ongoing overnight rain and we were woken in early hours by my mother-in-law's hysterical calls. We rushed downstairs to find the ground floor under a feet or more of water. There were obviously mopping up duties and insurance claims and low and behold the very same thing happened the following year.

She could turn her hand to most things and was skilled in dressmaking in which she was a perfectionist. Coincidently, at the time of writing, I can see out onto the street through the front bay window. Around that window is a pair of curtain and drapes the width of the living room and to her credit they were made from the skill of her hands.

As of mine the family I was marrying into were of working class and proud of the fact. Whatever job needed doing it would be considered if it could be done by themselves first before calling in a tradesman. It would be many years before we were to call in a

225

painter and decorator as we all 'mucked in' as they say in the Black Country.

They lived in a council house with the kitchen window looking out onto the front garden and a smaller window by the sink on the side. The side door was used as the main entrance, directly through another and it was straight into the kitchen. It was a decent size with the normal kitchen appliances and a table and chairs underneath the front window where you could watch the world go by. Very often the Father-in-Law would be there with a newspaper open on the horse racing page. On the floor they had a small electric fire which was ideal for cooking toast. Most days would be spent in that room and the evenings in the living room. If looking from that window I would have been seen many times walking around that corner wearing the fashion of the day with big jacket collars and Solatio shoes.

"when yer Ma was in the kitchen cooking dinner
an' yer Da was in th' paper for a winner
on yer back door, tap tappin' one, two, three
that'll be me, that'll be me"

226

Having checked on the internet the spelling of the shoes I was amazed to see an almost identical pair for sale at an enormous amount on a well known site. This reminded me of when I kept a pair for best wear and meeting my dad for a pint in the Rough Hills Tavern. I was alarmed to look down to see that he was wearing them!

Late in life as far as buying a house goes my in-laws were to make the decision to do so. This would have been their home for two score years or more since moving here from the Bilston area and they wanted to own it.

Football had once again taken the front seat and weekends were spent playing and building a team spirit, some call it socialising. Training was spent one or two evenings a week for those who were fitness minded and being a keen runner it was always in my diary. Signing for Sedgley Rovers in the Wolverhampton Amateur League was a great decision as to this day I still look back in fondness of that time in my life.

Tenscore, Sedgley, 2014

"I made my home début
on the Tenscore,
admiring the Staffordshire,
Shropshire view.
The old colliery land of Baggeridge,
Wombourne and Himley too"

I Once Was a Sedgley Rover ©

2007

Old team photos remind me of the day,
When I was younger and able to play.
All of the memories and friends that I made,
Wherever I chose to ply my trade.
Now it's all gone and it's over,
I once was a Sedgley Rover.
A name of respectable football recognition,
With history, style and tradition.

I made my home début on the Tenscore,
Admiring the Staffordshire, Shropshire view.
The old colliery land of Baggeridge,
Wombourne and Himley too.
The local amateur football scene was fantastic,
Socks around ankles,
Or tied up with tape or elastic.
This Black Country town and its people,
The pitch in the shadow of All Saints steeple.
This all made me proud to pull over,
The shirt of a Sedgley Rover.

Boarding the coach in the Bull Ring,
Saturday's here there's a venue to find.
The Rovers set off from Sedgley,
Leaving the height of the Beacon behind.
The White Horse pub for Tuesday meetings.
The Station Hotel in Dudley,
Presentation awards and greetings.

Harry Love, Sidney Partridge and Charlie Hale,
Gave me fond memories,
And I can still tell a tale.
About games that we won or we lost,
A referee and two captains
Without a coin to be tossed.
And now it's all gone and it's over,
I once was a Sedgley Rover.

Recently, at the time of writing, I received an e-mail from someone asking for information that I may have of my time at Bilston Town FC. He had visited my website and noticed I had mentioned having a spell there. After a rummage up in the loft for my scrapbook of paper cuttings I forwarded the following;

Throughout the 1975-76 when aged 21 whilst playing for Sedgley Rovers and a regular in the Wolverhampton Amateur League Select side, I was made aware that I had attracted the interest of Bilston Town FC. I had also been approached a couple times after games but declined to leave the Rovers.

One frosty Sunday morning fixture I suffered a shoulder injury after having an heavy fall on the hard surface. I was later to find out when returning to the pitch that it was a 'bit serious' and it was a broken collar bone.

Whilst first off the pitch a gentleman in a heavy duffle coat introduced himself. It was Alan Wakeman, Manager of Bilston Town. He had chosen to speak to me personally having declined earlier advances.

I cannot be sure at this point if it was before or after he had reported in the Pink of his 'extreme disappointment of me not signing for Bilston and that he thought I had tremendous potential'.

After a good 6 weeks being out and recovering from my shoulder injury, a letter from Mr Wakeman was awaiting when I arrived home from a meeting. He had chosen to speak to my wife to help encourage me to make the move. Reports in the Pink were that he had been 'chasing Bennett since the middle of last season'. Headlines were again in the pink saying that 'Bennett leaves Sedgley' as I signed for Bilston for season 1976-77.

It turned out to be another painful chapter of my footballing life as Mr Wakeman described me as 'being too brave for my own good' as I tried all I could to score goals.

My début was in a pre-season away game at Stratford and being a 5'10" forward and known as being 'good in the air' as they say, I was struck at the back of the head by the opposing centre-backs forehead. Stratford

Hospital awaited me with my nasty 2 inch gash of a skull injury. I can still recall drifting in and out of consciousness on a plastic sheet on a bed and the sash windows being open and the incoming summer breeze. Reports followed that 'Bennett goes to Hospital' and that I had suffered an eye injury! Other newspapers also got it wrong.

My comeback was on Queens Street in my one and only reserve game. In the second period and chasing my hat-trick, I was struck in the face by the goalkeepers elbow that broke my nose diagonally from the right eye socket to the left cheekbone. The Royal Hospital, Wolverhampton now awaited me!

Reports a week later; 'Despite a broken nose, striker Robbie Bennett played in Bilston's impressive 4-1 FA Cup win at VS Rugby'.

Said manager Alan Wakeman: "He was literally on his knees at the end of the match but his enthusiastic play had been a welcome sight."

I see in paper cuttings that I have that I had scored two headed goals, one in each half, in Bilston's 2-0 FA Trophy tie against Brereton. Unfortunately my head injuries had taken their toll and Alan Wakeman tried his best to keep me, but to no avail, proving that he was genuine in his opinion that I had potential. I had scored about half a dozen goals so far and at the time I was top scorer but my Bilston days were over.

On a happier note, scoring all 4 goals, two goals in
each half of a 2-2 draw in a practice game with Mr
Wakeman swapping me over at half-time. He followed
that up by bringing to me a glass of whisky whilst I
was showering but by the end of the glass it had more
water in it than alcohol. Whenever at Queens Street
now, my memories come flooding back, especially the
goal area where I lay injured. I was in and out of
football for the next 24 years or so along with
marathon running. I gave back to the game by
coaching my son and team. My time at Bilston Town
Football Club was brief and painful and I most
probably will not be remembered but it is a huge part
of my football story.

Bilston Town Football Club,
Queen Street

"He 'deliberately done me'
as they say,
a hospital visit again that day,
who keeps the score
and chases the glory?
The bloke with the scars
who's telling the story"

My Bloody Bilston Début ©

2014

I can remember the old sash windows
Open in the warm summertime,
The blood that was on the plastic sheet
Wasn't his, wasn't yours but mine.

I can remember the slippers he wore
He playfully cursed as he walked through the door.
Called from watching golf on the telly,
And ready to feed his belly,

The hospital phoned to do a stitch-up job
Part of his duties to do this job,
In a semi-conscious state
Me, in a bed I did wait.

It happened in Stratford one summer
For Bilston in a pre-season match,
Near two score years have gone since then
Leaving a scar near my ageing bald patch

This conquer tree of a centre-half
Was surprised how high I could climb,
The blood that I said on the plastic sheet
Wasn't his, wasn't yours but mine.

Soon I was back regarded as fit
Good news you expect I suppose,
In my comeback I jumped for my hat-trick
And the goalkeeper broke my nose.

He 'deliberately done me' as they say
A hospital visit again that day,
Who keeps the score and chases the glory?
The bloke with the scars who's telling the story.

Now I'm not the type to say my time was better
That's not fair to the young in my book,
Encourage and teach don't bore them and preach
What they need is a good stroke of luck.

In October of 1976 a relation of ours named Willie was over from Canada. This one night we all went out for a drink in the New Inn. It is located in the Monmore Green area of Wolverhampton where the Steelway and Laystall works are. In recent years the Metro line to Wolverhampton and Birmingham has been operating.

I recall Willie being very smart in his suit and tie and with a smiling face and a gentle nature. Looking back it must have been a unique visit from Willie and our dad was chuffed that he had a relative staying there. While I was buying a round of drinks at the bar I could hear the fight start between Joe Bugner and Richard Dunne. I took two or three drinks over to family who were sitting at a table and returned to the bar for the remaining glasses. By the time I had got back to the bar there had been a first round knock out and the fight was over.

The Bilston Road for us kids from the Rough Hills was a kind of boundary. Beyond that boundary was the road to the East Park where they had a band stand and a paddling pool. Before all that was the Speedway where we could hear the roars of the bikes. The last time I was in the New Inn there were pictures relating to the Speedway on the wall.

During Willie's stay in Wolverhampton we also had a get together at the Butlers Arms where a relation on my mothers side was the licensee. The pub has long been demolished and a supermarket now occupies the land. At the time I was working with my old pal Len (see Old Len Muir Was Funny) who also had relations living in Toronto. I introduced Len to Willie and if my memory serves me correct Willie knew them and he was their breadman.

Upon researching family members about Willie's visit, Joan in Louisiana informed me he had lived in Canada since 1953 and that it was she who gave him our address in England and he was glad that he had came.

The New Inn, Bilston Road, 2013

"A Banks's pub was the New Inn
at the bottom of Dixon Street,
there once was a traffic island there
where the Ettingshall
and Bilston Road does meet"

OUR WILLIE ©

2010

We went for a drink with our Willie
Down Monmore Green one night,
Willie was over from Toronto
On the radio that night was a heavyweight fight.

A Banks's pub was the New Inn
At the bottom of Dixon Street,
There once was a traffic island there
Where the Ettingshall and Bilston Road does meet.

At the bar we were when the bout begun
Joe Bugner was fighting Richard Dunne,
For the British Heavyweight Title crown
Dunne in the first round defeated and down.

Nineteen seventy six
And because of that fight I remember the night
When we went for a drink with our Willie
Times flying by all right.

Trams are now back in fashion
And the island it is no more,
The Metro does make a commuting snake
A few yards from the New Inn door.

And I always think of our Willie
When I'm driving by in my car,
Yes I always think of that night with our Willie
And Bugner and Dunne at the bar.

We lived with my wife's parents in their house in Parkfields for a couple of years before being allocated the top dwelling of a two-storey maisonette just around the corner. Almost 6 years into our marriage we became proud parents of a baby girl. She was later to have a pretty dark haired daughter who is much like her in many ways.

Her Little Lips ©

2007

Her little lips were like pencil lines on a picture,
Her little fingers were too small to be real,
I was encouraged to touch them and feel.

Her little grip wrapped around my little finger,
Magnetically drawing me in,
The man meant to be then ended,
Or did the man meant to be, begin?

After a few years living in the flat we made the
important decision of looking for a house to buy. We
made an offer that was accepted on a semi-detached
house at the rear of the Parkfield Tavern. This would
be the last pub that I was to have a drink with my
Grandad. It was at this house that we became proud
parents again of our second child, a son who was very
near to being born in Blackpool with my wife having
to spend a weekend in the maternity unit there. It was
the time of the ambulance strike and calls back home
to my family was that the baby was going to be born
there. Things changed and we were allowed to travel
home with a list of hospitals on route if needed.

We invested in the house by alterations and double
glazing etcetera and upon selling it later we found that
we had only broke even. Nevertheless we improved the
house all round and made a safe garden for the
children to play in. Two people from Codsall, Mick
Perry our Co-op Insurance Man and Tony Doody a
Plaster and cousin of my brother-in-law, who done
work on the house, were to kick-start my footballing
life in later years.

I have a great memory of my dad and myself in about 1983 laying turf. Here is my poem for those who have lost a parent and wish they could meet them later on in life. My dad helped me lay the back lawn in this, the first house that we bought. He didn't live to help me on our second. He was rolling his fag's with his soiled fingers and there was more dirt than tobacco as he had ran low.

A Fifty Something Me ©

2010

I would have loved my old man to meet me now
And see a fifty something me
A twenty something me could climb a tree
Green the grass oh green it shall grow
A fifty something me

He helped me lay turf where my bairns first played
He helped me lay the turf
Green the grass oh green it shall grow
He rolled tobacco in God's earth
With a twenty something me

I would have loved my old man to meet me now
And see a fifty something me
A thirty something me could climb a tree
A thirty something me

I would have loved my old man to meet me now
And see a fifty something me
Green the grass oh green it shall grow

A fifty something somebody
A fifty something me

I would have loved my old man to meet me now
And help me lay a lawn
Green the grass oh green it shall grow
How green the grass that's born

I was well and truly focused in those days in being a provider, home builder, husband and parent. I was never a great scholar nor was I a master craftsman but I could graft and my wife proved to be the expert with our finances.

A Man Should Earn ©

2008

A man should earn his pound and packet of pay.
He should prioritise the importance
of earning every single day.
Especially when there are bairns to feed
those who have the most need.
A man should earn his pound and packet of pay.
He should prioritise the importance
of spending every single day.
If he don't earn he don't spend,
he don't steal he don't lend.
A man should step forth and accept responsibility,
Not hand me downs and expecting life to be free.
When work has dried at least he tried.
And tomorrow shall try some more
else the wolf shall appear at his door.
He should prioritise the importance
of earning every single day,
A man should earn his pound and packet of pay.

Self-explanatory, a man should earn and face up to his responsibilities. It's unhealthy to the mind of man to laze their days away when there are bills to be paid and mouths to be fed. Some men get on the downward spiral and find it hard to get off.

"he should prioritise the importance of earning every single day"

A house over the road from where we live in 2012 has been sold and for a few weeks now there has been plenty of activity work wise. This reminded me of when we were young parents at our old house, working towards being in the living room at Christmas. The house really was like a building site and our first child grew to accepting it as normal.

I worked a full day and hours in the evening at home to prepare the house as it was more like a building site. This one year I was working like balmy to be in the living room by Christmas Day and we succeeded.

"workin' every day for pay
toilin' on the house at night"

My Christmas Paper Chain ©

2012

A child to guard and shield, in our house at
Beaconsfield
we had our work cut out did we,
let's be living in the living room by Christmas
seemed the slightest possibility.

Workin' every day for pay
toilin' on the house at night,
because the living room was not a living room
downright more like beyond a building site.

'decorating Christmas, with a paper chain to last,
my Yuletide paper chain of people and past'.

Walls patched up and plastered
we mastered many a chore,
counting the days of December
it was nearing twenty four.

Soon the paper had paste upon
that patched up plastered wall,
and carpet was laid down on
boards on the living room floor.

'decorating Christmas, with a paper chain to last,
my Yuletide paper chain of people and past'.

Breaking up at dinnertime
I cycled home on Christmas Eve,
no time yet for festivity
I came in and rolled up my sleeve.

A child to guard and shield, in our house at
Beaconsfield
we had our work cut out did we,
the living room was now a living room that Christmas
there ends that part of my Christmas tale to thee.

'decorating Christmas, with a paper chain to last,
my Yuletide paper chain of people and past'.

Another child to guard and shield, in our house at
Beaconsfield,
then we moved on homes did we,
still living in our living room at Christmas
and time moves rapidly.

Come on grandchildren come on,
you're on my paper chain,
get your crayons, pens and pencils,
scribble faces and write your name,
link again on my Christmas paper chain.

'decorating Christmas, with a paper chain to last,
an 'auld strang' paper chain,
my Yuletide paper chain of people and past',
Grandad Robbie's Christmas paper chain!

Within 40 yards of our house at the rear of the
Parkfield Tavern the runners on the Wolverhampton
Marathon passed by like a long snake. The following
year of 1984 it had my name on the finishing list that
was printed a day or two later in the Express and Star.
I had been training hard on a Thursday evening at
John Thompson Sports Ground for a couple of years
with a few mates and it seemed the obvious next step.
A runner in 1983 was one of our training mates and
marathons were to take over my life for the next few
years.

We Couldn't Catch Ray!©

2010

Never minding the sleet or rain
at John Thompson's we would train,
young me an' few others, with the Hale brothers,
looking back I'd probably say, we couldn't catch Ray!

Week by week the fitter we'd get,
pumping up muscle and building up sweat.
Sit-ups an' press-ups a plenty,
sometimes running on empty,
young me an' few others, with the Hale brothers,
looking back I'd probably say, we couldn't catch Ray!

Just a few blokes with passion and desire
burning off fat, stoking up the fire
putting more fuel in the tank
running around trees up the sports ground bank
young me an' few others, with the Hale brothers,
looking back I'd probably say, we couldn't catch Ray!

We turned up at Thompson's in our training kit
but we never caught Ray 'cause he was too damn fit,
every Thursday we'd attend
good times, a shame it had to end
young me an' few others, with the Hale brothers,
looking back I'd probably say, we couldn't catch Ray!

Poem written on a Thursday after attending Ray's funeral.

I was as proud as punch in 1984 when the marathon route took us down Dixon Street and past the road where I grew up in. Mother and neighbours were waving and shouting and it lifted the spirit. Another memory is seeing my dad on the Wellington Road nearing the bottom of Wolverhampton Street. Years later I still see him there today and shall see him there the next time I drive by.

For me it was just over 3 hours to the finish line on the hill of the Ring Road where my wife and children were calling me on by the Molineux Hotel. In October of that year we were to travel down to relations in Harlow, Essex for yet another marathon and we have a picture of my daughter with me as I ran over the finishing line. There are also pictures of my young son hanging out of the stationary car window on the route.

I had turned 30 of that year and my younger brother had to get me out of the house as a surprise party was planned. I thought it was odd as he was not yet a runner but off we went for a quick, or not so fast 5 miler. When we arrived back I noticed a few cars parked outside of our house. Much to my delight it was a lovely surprise but for the cursing of my brother who was complaining that he had no choice but to take me for a run as I didn't play darts!

When I was a young lad I was Alf Tupper 'The Tough of the Track'. If you are roughly the same age as me you will know him as a comic hero. He was a schoolboy runner who was as honest as the day is born and worked hard for everything he achieved. I don't know who created Alf but I wonder if he knew how many youngsters that he inspired.

In the mid eighties I am working at Narrow Aisle UK a forklift company and I am in conversation with Alan 'George' Rudge. He is Alan because that is what his mother wanted him named and George because that is what his dad wanted him called. It is most confusing when he explains this to you but he has 'Alan' tattooed on his arm, or is it 'George?

One day Rudgie and I were talking about great sportsmen and I mentioned Alf Tupper and the surprise on his face when he realised that he also inspired him. The following Sunday morning we had arranged to play football over Caswells in Parkfields and from the top of a hill I could hear a voice calling me. There was Rudgie proudly wearing his new tee shirt with the logo that he had printed on 'Alf Tupper Lives OK'.

In 2002, my old poem of Alf was printed in The Black Country Bugle and I dedicated it to Rudgie and he was told of it while he was at work at Goodyears. I was beginning to think that he did not know of it but a phone call one evening a few weeks later from my brother surprised me. "Hello Rob I'm at the fair and someone wants to speak to you". " Hi'ya Bob" a voice called "Alf Tupper lives ok", "he certainly does", I replied.

Years later when working elsewhere a colleague of mine was a former well known pro-footballer. One of his clubs was West Bromwich Albion. He surprisingly told me that Alf Tupper was his idol as a young lad. From that conversation I later presented him with a copy of my poem.

Alf Tupper lives in the heart of a generation of young boys, me included.

ALF TUPPER

THE TOUGH OF THE TRACK ©

1997

He lived on fish and chips suppers,
Who did? Alf Tupper,
The Tough Of The Track.

A runner from birth,
The salt of the earth.
Alf Tupper,
The Tough Of The Track.

A high school boy he was not,
He didn't get
What the other kid's got.

264

They laughed in his face
When they lined up to race.
Alf Tupper,
The Scruff Of The Track.

Now Alf he ran from the heart,
Gone like a flash at the start.
He battled the best,
And he'd beat the rest.
Alf Tupper,
The Tough of the Track.

Alf at the time was a tonic,
You forgot he only lived in a comic.
But look in your mind,
Inside you may find,
Alf Tupper,
The Tough of the Track.

Well settled and into family life, simple ways, home loving days and the children came first. My dad had died but their remaining three Grandparents were proud of them and it showed.

I was, and still am a family man and proud of my children and the parents of what they became.

Beaconsfield Avenue, Parkfields, 1983

*"To know what you have
and how much do you need,
how strong is the envy
that turns into greed?"*

MY FAMILY MY TREASURE ©

2003

My word is my strength
And my voice speaks the truth,
My children are memories
That reminds me of youth.

My eyes see the danger
That they cannot see,
I've taught them their wisdom
But do they believe me?

To forgive their wrong doing
But needing to scold,
My arms wrapped around them
When they've felt the cold.

Some may be richer
In fortune or wealth,

Others are poorer
With sadness or health.

To know what you have
And how much do you need,
How strong is the envy
That turns into greed?

I've felt the pleasure
And I've shed the tears,
My family my treasure
That's built upon years.

It saddens me that my children did not know their Scottish Grandad in the prime of his life but there was no complaining of their other. We lived just over a mile away from my daughters school and it was important for him to get her home safe.

My Gag ©

1991

I've got a grandad
I call Gag,
He's got a nickname
We call Hag.

He's been my best friend
All my life,
Oh! By the way
Olive's his wife.

He was in the Air Force
In the war,
Keeping the enemy
From our door.

When I think of my Gag
I'm so proud,
But when I'm naughty
He shouts loud.

He tells me to be careful
He tells me to be good,
He tells me to behave myself
Like all kids should.

He meets me after school
In his Blue Allegro car,
He drives me home safe
Even though it's not far.

Now I'm sitting quiet
He has just said,
Come on little girl
Off to bed.

I can recall one holiday moment in the upstairs terrace of a pub in Borth when I took a wonderful, simple photograph of Grandfather and Grandson relationship. I could not have asked for anyone better to love my children on my own father's behalf.

With Love And With Pride ©

2006

My son he always kept his eyes on, he was there for
him day and night,
When we went for a ride to the club or seaside, he kept
him within his sight.

My son he sat down on a step at Borth, his Grandad sat
there by his side,
While my son sat down on a step at Borth,
His Grandad watched over with love and with pride.

A great childhood I had and I was doing my utmost to see that my children had one also. I built whatever I could like my dad did for us and everything was geared up for our children as they were in the forefront of my mind. I can recall my answer to a question at work one day that "I was the man that I had always wanted to be". I wished for nothing else than health and happiness for my family.

The Sand of Life ©

2004

Sometimes in my daydream
At a peaceful time,
I wonder into my own life
Inside this mind of mine.

Winters and a snowman
Our sledges on the slopes,
Swings down on the playground
Held by chains or ropes.

Sometimes in my daydream
Ah! my first bike,
Shop window on my birthday
Choose anything I like.

Toy soldiers in their uniform
A cowboy on his horse,
Which one does the hero ride?
The white one yes of course.

Sometimes in my daydream
I think about this land,
My precious childhood holidays
Sun, seaside and the sand.

We went to Lowestoft
Watching fishermen birth,
Their catch lay fresh and helpless
Fishmongers priced their worth.

Sometimes in my daydream
Recalling what I've seen,
All my lifetime memories
Everywhere I've been

The pleasant land of Worcestershire
When driving to the south,
The Avon and when crossing
Over the river mouth.

The Highlands and the Borders
Castles and their land,
There's so much for us all to learn
That we don't understand.

Sometimes in my daydream
The sand of life falls from my hand,
Schooling comes too early
There's so much history in our land.

Our land, so much history in our land
That we don't understand.

Bilston is 2 miles southeast of Wolverhampton well known for its market; iron works and has a coal mining history. A typical example of a small Black Country town, although the borough of Bilston ceased in the 1960's it has kept its own identity. The 'Stump' mentioned in the 4th verse of my next ode is the name that locals call the Swan Bank Tavern public house. It also has a football team; Bilston Town founded in 1894 as Bilston FC and nicknamed the Steelmen. Their ground is Queen Street and I had a spell there, as mentioned, in the 1970's when they played in the West Midlands League. They have in recent years fell on hard times and almost folded. New owners reformed them as Bilston Town (2007)

Sunday morning July 26, 2009 my wife and I decided to drive to Bilston to take photographs to display on this page. It was apparent that times have changed but nevertheless at least we came. Firstly, we noticed the Swan Bank Tavern was yet another pub struggling with the modern age, boarded up and for sale. We strolled around the back of the pub to Bow Street where her dad had lived but it is now mainly new buildings and a car park. My wife felt quite sad about losing part of her past and even suggested, tongue in cheek for us to buy the pub. We then crossed the road and made our way to St Leonard's Church. It was here she remarked where she was baptised. For the first time we saw Witness, the work of Bettina Furnee, quotes in iron castings from people of Bilston and the industrial change.

We still have a picture on our wall of my wife's Grandfather. He was standing in a group-wedding photo which had been zoomed in to make an individual picture. Later back at home we studied the doorway in the background and little had changed except wear and tear and 2 pillars were not there. We could still make out the writing overhead, RESTORED ANNO DOMINI 1883. When taking the photograph I had in mind I was in the same viewpoint that the photographer of that day was in and imagined my wife's family being pictured.

We then went back to the car looking at the war memorial on route and drove to the other end of Bilston where my mother-in law had grew up. The buildings including her home in Wolverhampton

Street have long since gone with only over grown land in view.

I often look at landscape and skyline and many times it has got me back on track before the age of sat nav. I'm greatly interested in buildings, places and people who lived there in their given day. In my youthful day my approach to Bilston was down the Parkfield and Millfield Road. At that entrance is now a modern island with a structure of today. That structure would be alien to my mother-in- law's age but the landscape and the odd building remains.

There is a Sure Start Nursery building over the road that she assures was known as the 'Mission'. In front of what is now the Nursery was the Chapel but now long gone. My wife and I studied the design in the brickwork of the Nursery building wondering if that was actually the Chapel but informed not.

The front of their house over the road from the Chapel was used as a barbershop where her dad cut hair for half a penny. Accordingly there were three public houses in the vicinity. The Barrel on the corner of Mill Street, the Hand and Bottle and the Hand and Keys. Her relations also owned a sweet shop on Wolverhampton Street known as Tandy's.

St Leonard's, Bilston, 2012

"Apparent in her accent
anyone can tell,
her folks they came from Bilston
she is my Bilston belle"

My Bilston Belle ©

2009

Her folks they came from Bilston
deep Black Countrified,
she kept the place they came from
her roots she did not hide.

Apparent in her accent
anyone can tell,
her folks they came from Bilston
she is my Bilston belle.

Her folks they came from Bilston
salt of the earth is often said,
her mom was raised in a barber shop
hair cut and shred from a Bilston head.

Her dad once lived behind the 'Stump'
I know for he once did tell,
her folks they came from Bilston
she is my Bilston belle.

Her folks they came from Bilston
deep Black Countrified,
they then moved on to Bradley
not far to walk or ride.

Moved and schooled in Parkfields
She turned out well
Her folks they came from Bilston
she is my Bilston belle.

Her folks they came from Bilston
market, steelworks and moulding,
everything is changing
shops and factories folding.

It's hard to change as a person
do I need to tell?
Her folks they came from Bilston
she is my Bilston belle.

My bonnie Bilston beauty
She turned out well
Her folks they came from Bilston
she is my Bilston belle.

285

I'm often around the Rough Hills and wonder if there are others who think like I do of the old days? The Rough Hills Tavern and the Moulders Arms or Monkey House as it is well known, are both boarded up and it's sad to see. There is football on Dixon Street playing field but not on Rooker Avenue. In our young day we could sit on the Tavern wall and see two games at a time. It was directly behind the goal of the one pitch so we had to keep watch as a miss hit shot frightened many a drinker when the ball smacked the bar window.

Thinking of this time in my life reminds me of a certain local footballer and a good one at that. I first saw Roger Salter playing football in Parkfields on a Saturday afternoon on Rooker Avenue playing field. Later in life we were to work and play in the same team together. This one evening we were out socialising and he stopped by at our house for a night-cap. I was reminded of this evening by his wife Pat when paying my last respect for him and of a poem I wrote about 28 years previously called Roger an Innocent Man.

I had forgot about the poem but not the evening as
Roger said that he knew he had had too much to drink
as he had just saw a 'rat in a bubble'. It was actually a
hamster in an exercise ball that I had just put down.

I had wrote the poem in humour for Roger being late
home. Little did I know that over the years they both
had many a laugh about it. Upon realizing I was there
on the day of Roger's funeral, Pat sent someone back to
their house to get the poem. There it was, hand
scribbled on an ageing piece of notepad paper.

Rooker Avenue Playing Fields, 2013

"he trapped, sprayed a pass
call it whatever
but for now
...I'll call it world class
thinking of all I can
of Roger Salter
an innocent man"

Roger Salter, an Innocent Man ©

2012

In football terms
two footed
jumped like a salmon
and I am
thinking of all I can
of Roger Salter
an innocent man

he trapped, sprayed a pass
call it whatever
but for now
...I'll call it world class
thinking of all I can
of Roger Salter
an innocent man

around five feet nine
maybe touching five feet ten
defending in a team
against rugged, tough men
thinking of all I can
of Roger Salter
an innocent man

Parkfield Working Mens I think
the club for he was playing
where my old man had a drink
thinking of all I can
of Roger Salter
an innocent man

I could spot him everywhere
closing down forwards
with his long dark hair
thinking of all I can
of Roger Salter
an innocent man

Rooker Avenue was the pitch
playing for love and not to get rich

thinking of all I can
of Roger Salter
an innocent man

sticking out
and getting stuck in
giving tricky players nowt
and out to get a win
thinking of all I can
of Roger Salter
an innocent man

in a cloudy white field
up in the sky
is many a player
that will never ever die
and there is one
that's leaping like a salmon
two footed
and I'm gutted
thinking of all I can
of Roger Salter
an innocent man

It was a surprise one morning in late May 2013 to open an e-mail with a small poem about me and the mention of the Bugle?

At first I was a bit bemused but after a short while the penny dropped that there may be a piece of my writing in the Black Country Bugle. With that in mind I went up to the local paper shop and purchased the latest edition. It was around 1995 that I first had a poem printed in The Bugle and the same excitement came over me as it did then. If it was a poem, I could not think what it could be as I had not sent anything in recent weeks. There it was on page 14, my ode about Roger Salter, and I was delighted to see an old mates name in print. Our playing and working together days came flooding back.

I have re-read the poem a few times since it being in print and thought that it needed a picture or two. Whilst next in the area I parked up in Rooker Avenue and took a photo of where the pitch was when I first saw Roger. Yes I was correct, I could visualise him with his long hair, which was the fashion of the day, closing down forwards and leaping high to beat them in the air. He really was two-footed and it is a credit to Roger that you could not tell which one. It was a Sunday and most disappointingly there was not one youngster playing on the field. Roger and I were of a different generation and football pitches were the only places to be.

Standing there alone I turned around to see the derelict Rough Hills Tavern. I looked for the outdoor entrance where many times us kids would be hanging about. I've returned many a bottle to the Tavern to get my 3d's. I can also remember my dad being bitten by the landlord's dog as he was walking across the car-park.

Rough Hills Tavern, 2008
demolished 2014

*"I can see my father laughing
in the tavern,
although the lovely Tavern,
it is no more"*

LAUGHING IN THE TAVERN ©

2014

I can see my father laughing
in the Tavern,
see others throwing darts there
at the board,
I can see my father laughing
in the Tavern,
whilst domino players are knocking,
dancers are rolling and rocking,
to music coming from the concert room,
folk so happy in the Tavern
they're over the moon.

At the outdoor kids are queuing
for crisps and pop is what they're doing,
and laughing in the passage
of the Tavern.

A pint in hand,
going to listen to the band,
the singer in the Tavern sounds so grand,
singing in the Tavern with 'mic' in hand.

I can see my father laughing
in the tavern,
although the lovely Tavern,
it is no more,
I shall see my father laughing,
laughing in the Tavern,
The Rough Hills Tavern
laughing in the Tavern for evermore.

My next stop was not far away at Martin Street to take a photo of Parkfields Working Mens Club. That did not appear to be open so I wondered if it is another social venue that has gone. I recalled that it had a bowling green at the rear of the club that you could access in the next street and I found it to be overgrown. In 1986 we had moved to the other side of Wolverhampton, although pleased to be in my old area, I was saddened of the times of change as we had many happy hours at the club and on the playing field. To recall people and places to mind makes a life worth living.

Martin Street, Parkfields, 2013

We left behind us venues of where we met and
courted and little did we know at the time that most
would be closed in the future. The Red Lion on
Parkfield Road, Union Mill and Bulls Head on the
lights by John Thompson's where they had the
occasional disco's, The Fighting Cocks, all places we
socialised in our young life. We were only moving a
15–20 minute drive away but it may have been to
another country as many people we knew have not
been seen since. Another country was calling as
Scottish ancestral feelings inside of me were gaining
strength.

Ettingshall Lights, 2014

"Bilston and Millfields
the children came,
when the Fair came
to Parkfield Road,
to Parkfield Road the Fair came"

My Beautiful Queen ©

2009

She's wore my ring she has
For near on forty years
I've been her king I have
Often been her clown
She's wore my ring she has
For near on forty years
As her king I have
Tried not to let her down

I was her knight I was
Shining armour there were none

I was her prince I was
Near forty years have gone

The clown or king I am
Those forty years have seen
A pretty little princess
Become my beautiful queen

My beautiful queen our ageless love
Were you sent to me from heaven above?
From that Tuesday everything grew
Our courtship and wedding day
The words of I do

My pretty little princess
Still wears my ring
The music the melodies
Songs we did sing

I am her clown I am
Who thinks he is king.
My pretty little princess
She still wears my ring.

I was working as a Fork Lift Truck Fitter at Narrow Aisle UK when serious with my running. When I first joined the company it was off the Millfields Road by Stewart and Lloyds until moving to the old bus station on Mount Pleasant at the other side of Bilston. Most mornings I would run the two and a half mile to work down Dixon Street and the Wellington Road. This short run improved my race time dramatically. Very soon other work mates got their running shoes on including both my brothers as we all worked at the same place.

I miss those running days and the benefit of the general fitness that it gave but I must admit that it has taken its toll on my knees. Nevertheless I wish that I could turn back the sporting clock and play a game of football on our field and run once more down Dixon Street in the marathon.

To conclude this story, in 1986 we entered into a new chapter in our life by selling our house and moving to Codsall on the other side of Wolverhampton near to the Staffordshire and Shropshire border. We felt it was right for us as a family. It was then time to start all over again with the house development and once again we became the new neighbours.

So step by step, year by year it was awa' th' Rough Hills an' awa' and with my family I ventured into a new beginning.

Wee Robie still has a scar and not the pedal car he had for Christmas.

I Am Me And Not Another ©

2005

Wolverhampton and Scottish roots
Running shoes and football boots,
Seaside breeze and hillside views
A pint of beer and sporting news.
Who have I grown up to be?
Should I be another instead of me,
Do I take what not is mine?
Should I walk the dishonest line?
I'd rather settle for what I've got
Will I miss what I have not?
Satisfaction is guaranteed
My plate is full but not with greed.
A lifeline that was gave to me
And who that I have grown to be,

305

I am me and not another
A husband and son, a father and brother.
I've pushed a pen and wore toe-capped boots
I love my family and my roots,
Someday my time on earth will come
Then in the heavens again I'll run.
Over clouds and pass by far
The biggest brightest shining star.

Dixon St, at Cheviot Road

Wolverhampton Marathon

1985

The Author, dark kit to the right on the middle of the road.

All three Bennett boys from the Rough Hills ran and finished.....

For my family
(and now my bonnie Grandchildren)

"Lang may yer lum reek"

Made in the USA
Charleston, SC
19 September 2016